"In this fresh take on whole-parish involvement in the RCIA process, Diana Macalintal draws upon her pastoral ministry in a variety of settings and her life experience, inviting us to consider whether RCIA takes place 'in front of' or 'within' our parish community. Diana provides ample material for theological reflection, but also concrete suggestions to enrich any parish's initiation ministry. Appropriate for the seasoned veteran or the 'neophyte' to Christian Initiation, *Your Parish Is the Curriculum* will be a valued text for all who accompany new Christians on their faith journey."

> —Jeremy Helmes, Author of *Three Great Days*; Board of Directors, National Association of Pastoral Musicians; Pastoral Associate for Worship & Sacraments, St. Maximilian Kolbe Parish, Cincinnati, Ohio

"Often forgotten in discussions of evangelization is the role of the parish in forming a new way of life. Diana Macalintal's description of the parish as the curriculum for the RCIA serves as a medicine against this amnesia about the parish. Readers will discover in this book not simply an introduction to the role of the parish in the RCIA. They'll also learn a deeper appreciation for the way that the parish is the curriculum for formation in mature Christianity. Macalintal's book is an important contribution for those involved in adult formation, catechesis, and evangelization."

> —Timothy P. O'Malley, Academic Director, Notre Dame Center for Liturgy

"Have you felt daunted at fully implementing the Rite of Christian Initiation of Adults in your parish? When you finish Diana Macalintal's book, you'll wonder why you worried. *Your Parish Is the Curriculum* is a readable, concise, realistic, invigorating view of the entire formation and celebration of the RCIA. Whether you are new or experienced in this ministry, you will find fresh ideas and gain total confidence in the joyful task of helping interested adults join the Catholic family."

—Fr. Paul Turner
    Pastor, Cathedral of the Immaculate Conception,
        Kansas City, Missouri
    Director, Office of Divine Worship,
        Diocese of Kansas City-St. Joseph
    Author of various theological and pastoral resources

"In *Your Parish* Is *the Curriculum: RCIA In the Midst of the Community* Diana Macalintal offers a practical and engaging vision for parishes as communities of discipleship that accompany people at all stages of their faith journey through the Rite of Christian Initiation of Adults. In an accessible and down-to-earth manner she outlines principles, suggestions, and ideas to help parishes—both those who are new to the RCIA process and those who are veterans—to facilitate and foster conversion."

—Julianne Stanz
    Director of New Evangelization
    Diocese of Green Bay

Your Parish *Is* the Curriculum

RCIA in the Midst of the Community

Diana Macalintal

LITURGICAL PRESS
Collegeville, Minnesota

www.litpress.org

For Nick, who taught me to ask, "What if?"

Contents

Introduction

Rocio

I didn't know everything would change for our community the moment the doorbell rang. The receptionist was on vacation that week, and it was my turn to sit at her desk at the Catholic Newman Center where I worked. The university's January term had just begun, and I expected to see yet another wayward student looking for Mass or confession.

"Hi. Is this a church?" she asked when I answered the door.

Her voice sounded tiny and apprehensive, like many college freshmen sound when they come to church for the first time on their own. But she didn't look like most of the young students we encountered. Her lips were ruby red, but everything else about her was clothed in black. Her jet-black hair matched the thick line of midnight-black eyeliner that defined her eyes. Black nail polish and leather bands marked her fingers and wrists. (We'd later learn that the bands were there to hide the scars.) Chunky black boots, jeans, and a black T-shirt finished the ensemble. She was the perfect model for those who saw the world as dark and their place in it as outcast.

"Yes! This is the Catholic Center," I answered, hoping I sounded reassuring. "Do you want to come in?" I asked, opening the door wider.

She peeked behind me into the dim vestibule before she replied in a shaky voice, "Yeah. I think I want to get baptized."

That was the beginning of our community's journey with Rocio. But it hadn't been the beginning of her journey of faith. She had already traveled a long and unhappy road to get there. Bad friendships had led to abusive relationships, and people she thought would have her back had abandoned her. Those who stayed taught her to doubt herself and her own worth, which made it easier for her to accept the abuse. No wonder she clothed herself in darkness; it was all she knew.

Yet, something else also led her to that door. As people of faith, we would call it God's grace. Rocio knew it as an ache for something better, something more. Thank God, she believed this was the place to find it. As she stepped into the entryway, I sensed it was an act of hope—for her and for us—to say yes to this new relationship.

God at Work

Rocio joined us every Sunday for Mass. She was painfully shy at first, so we put together a small group of people who took turns sitting with her each Sunday and hanging out with her after Mass during coffee and donuts. At Mass she enjoyed the singing, but she couldn't quite figure out the standing and sitting and kneeling or the responses. We told her just to do what we did, and she'd be fine. With the help of her new companions, she began meeting a few other community members. Most of them were students like her, but there were also a lot of other people from the neighborhood and alumni who had never left.

Slowly, she began to open up and started asking lots of questions: What does it mean when you put your hand in that water and touch your forehead? Why do you change all the colors in the church every few weeks? Where do those readings come from? How do you know all the responses? How do you become a reader? Who are these statues? We'd all answer her questions as best as we could.

As she became more comfortable with us, we began to ask her a few questions of our own: What made you decide to come here?

Where have you been in your life? Are you happy? What do you hope for? What do you long for? Rocio told us that no one had ever asked her those kinds of questions before, and she was eager to discover the answers for herself.

Soon enough, little by little, we started noticing a bit of a change in Rocio. She wasn't as shy as she used to be and began to open up a bit more. She even volunteered to distribute the worship aids before Mass and greet people at the door. She didn't say much to them, but with those big ruby-red lips she smiled at every person.

Later that summer, she joined our annual student trip to Tijuana to an orphanage the students visit. They help the staff make repairs to the building and cook the meals. Mostly they play soccer with the kids or take turns giving piggyback rides in the dusty yard. It was here that we saw a completely different Rocio. She was vivacious and outgoing with the older kids, attentive and tender with the younger ones. She told the funniest jokes that made both the kids and adults topple over in laughter. Each evening, when we would sing and pray with the children, she made sure the littlest ones made the sign of the cross over themselves.

When she came back to school that fall, we noticed an even greater change in her. The heavy darkness that had once clothed her had given way to a budding joy, and there was a calmness to her spirit. She told us that her week with the kids at the orphanage had given her immense happiness. She wanted to change her life and help others like her be happy too. We knew she was ready to take that first public step toward what she had first asked for.

She became a catechumen a few weeks later and immersed herself into everything the Newman Center community was doing. There was a Tuesday night Bible study, and she and her sponsor—a friend she had made at the Newman Center—spent many hours in prayer and discussion with that group. Her many questions challenged everyone there to be more prepared. Some Fridays, they joined a group of students who rented movies to watch on the community TV. Each month, we served meals at a local women's shelter, and Rocio was always one of the first to sign up to serve. There was a rosary group that met in the dorm where Rocio lived, and she grew to love the rhythm of the prayers and the sincerity of those who prayed it. And Rocio never missed an opportunity to go back to Tijuana and be with those kids who had unlocked something in her that first summer. All the while, she and her sponsor were at Sunday Mass together, and we would meet with them and other catechumens for catechesis and fellowship.

Over the next few years, we saw wonderful changes in Rocio, but we also noticed changes in us. Having lived a difficult life with not-so-trustworthy friends, Rocio was never quick to accept everything she heard right away without some serious thought. So her questions for us became more and more discerning. Instead of just, "What does this mean?" she would ask, "Do you *really* believe that, and why?" Instead of "Who is Jesus?" or "Who is this saint?" she wanted to know, "Who is Jesus *for you*, and why does he matter *to you*?" These were questions with answers we wouldn't find in any book.

Rocio had once hidden behind the armor of her clothing. We realized that in some ways we, too, had been hiding behind the safety of our lesson plans, our catechisms, and our academically grounded notion that good research can find the answers to anything.

Rocio's presence and desire for living a true and honest Christian faith was gradually changing us into a community of people who had to be more intentional about what we believed and why. She wanted a community whose faith came not only from our head but more importantly from our heart. If we were to do that for Rocio, we needed to trust more in the slow and surprising work of the Holy Spirit than in our own sense of control. We had to listen more to the many places in our daily lives where God was speaking and not only to the experts among us who had prepared that week's presentation. Sometimes, we had no simple answers to her deepening questions because living out faith authentically isn't always so simple. Sometimes the only genuine answers we could give her were to pray more fervently, search for the truth together more humbly, and treat one another more compassionately.

Perhaps it was God's plan all along, but even as we tried to help Rocio grow in her own faith, it was she who helped us grow deeper in ours.

The Heart of Faith

After several years, all of us knew it was time for Rocio to receive what she had asked for that first day. That year's Easter Vigil was a cool, springtime evening. We had no formal chapel that could accommodate the entire community, so we held our Easter Vigil outside in the Newman Center backyard. We had built a makeshift font out of a horse trough and blue plastic tarp, with an army of lilies surrounding it. That afternoon, we filled the font with cold water from the garden hose. That night, under a recently full moon, Rocio stood alone in that font, with her godparent to her right and our pastor to her left. Their hands rested gently on her shoulders.

Into that dark night, our pastor asked Rocio, "Do you believe in God, the Father?" In a tiny voice that reminded me of our first conversation, Rocio whispered, "I do."

"Rocio, do you believe in Jesus, his only Son?" In a stronger voice came her reply, "I do."

Finally, he asked her, "Rocio, do you believe in the Holy Spirit?" Without prompting, she cried out in a voice I had never heard before, "I do with all my heart!" None of us were ready for it, that moment when all our hearts broke open to God's mysterious grace coming from this young woman.

Our pastor and Rocio's godparent gently lowered her down into that cold water and leaned her back a bit. Though his voice cracked with the love all of us were feeling, our pastor's voice resounded: "Rocio, I baptize you in the name of the Father . . ." They lowered her further into the water until her face was almost completely covered, then lifted her up. ". . . And of the Son . . ." Again, they submerged her lower still. As they brought her up again, I saw Rocio's face glistening and radiant. ". . . And of the Holy Spirit!" Down again they plunged her, and all of us held our breath with her. She came up the last time, dripping wet and crying, and we were crying too.

Right then, I knew that the person who had come up out of that water was not the same person I had met at that front door. The darkness that had made up so much of the old Rocio had been left behind in that font. The new Rocio standing before us, drenched with life and gleaming with light, was a completely brand-new creation.

There was something more. I realized that we who surrounded her that night were not the same community either. We had become more faithful and more true as Christians. The Gospel that for some of us had become rote and routine had come to life because of Rocio. No longer were we content with easy answers once we had learned to struggle together with Rocio's honest questions. Through it all, her sincere desire helped us never lose hope in Christ, in his church, or in one another. We had become more attentive to the Spirit's work and more obedient to the Spirit's movement at work in us and in the people who came to us seeking Christ. Everyone Rocio had touched—the Bible study group, the rosary group, the volunteers at the women's shelter and the orphanage, even the Friday night movie crowd—had grown deeper in their love for one another and in their faith in Christ because of Rocio's presence and participation in the life of the community. All of us had become more aware of how God was shaping our faith in our daily life together in study and prayer, in play and in service, and in joyful witness to the world. In that font, we, too, with Rocio, had been recreated into a more visible and merciful face of Christ.

What Really Happened

I want to tell you that *that* was exactly how it happened in that Newman Center almost thirty years ago. Mostly it was. But it wasn't because we planned it that way.

Our newly formed RCIA team was dead set on implementing our meticulously crafted and highly detailed catechetical formation calendar. The codirector and I had laid out the syllabus for the entire year. It was, of course, a September to May calendar because that's when the university was in session, even though the Newman Center had Sunday Mass and activities every week of the year.

We had assigned each of the thirty-two topics to the most theologically educated ones among our staff and team. They were to prepare their presentations, videos, and handouts for their assigned Wednesday night RCIA meeting. Each of those presentations were precisely timed to the gospels of each Sunday, and we double-checked the conversion schedule for when Rocio and all the other catechumens that year were supposed to be ready in order to be baptized that coming spring.

Poor Rocio and her sponsor! We required that both of them attend the Wednesday RCIA meeting every week, and if they didn't, we would do "make up" classes with them on Sunday. Because, really, if she didn't go to RCIA, when else would she learn about being Catholic?

Thank God that Rocio and the Holy Spirit weren't going to follow our schedule! The friends that Rocio made at the Newman Center, especially her sponsor, wanted her to be part of the community and do all the things the community did because it was simply what you did with your friends. It wasn't the RCIA team that encouraged her to go to Bible study. It was her sponsor because she was also a part of that group and thought Rocio would enjoy it too. In fact, the RCIA team was a bit annoyed with the Bible study group because Rocio would always come back from it excited with comments and questions about what she learned in Bible study, and her insights weren't fitting in with our topic that week. That first summer, while our RCIA team had been busy preparing the upcoming year's lesson plans, Rocio had gone to the orphanage in Tijuana because one of her new friends at the Newman Center was also going. Rocio found the rosary group herself because she saw a sign posted on the elevator at her dorm and was curious.

Now I'm sure that our weekly Wednesday night RCIA sessions were indeed forming Rocio in Catholic teaching, and she and her sponsor seemed to enjoy those gatherings. Moreover, that RCIA group of catechumens, candidates, and sponsors formed a tight-knit community, and we all came to know one another very deeply. Yet it was interesting to see that the year Rocio was initiated, only Rocio had stayed connected to the community after baptism. The other neophytes seemed to slowly disappear during that Easter season. We'd see them every so often on campus or at Sunday Mass. But only Rocio was consistently embedded (a good description for a neophyte, or "new plant") into the ongoing life of the community because she had planted roots within the community beyond our RCIA group. When we told the neophytes that they should go and be part of the wider community now that they were baptized and they didn't have to come to Wednesday night RCIA anymore, everyone protested, saying they would miss their RCIA gatherings. Only Rocio seemed unflustered. She was already making plans to start up a Wednesday night rosary group at her friend's dorm and had asked several other Newman Center folks to help out.

Neither Rocio nor the Holy Spirit was going to wait for the RCIA team to get her connected to the rest of the Body of Christ. To Rocio, the RCIA group was not the church; the entire Newman Center community was. And that community went beyond the walls of that building, all the way to the dormitories and the campus and the neighborhood. All the way to Tijuana. For Rocio, that Wednesday night RCIA gathering and everything she learned there only supplemented and enhanced the deeper learning of the Christian way of life that she was already living daily with her friends within the Christian community.

Have We Actually Tried the RCIA?

I've heard many RCIA team members confess to me how they felt they failed because a catechumen just never "got it." I've felt this too with other catechumens who didn't turn out to be as committed to discipleship as I hoped. I've shared war stories with pastors and RCIA directors about the "post-Easter drop-off," when many newly initiated slowly disappear. I've also heard from diocesan leaders and even some bishops the much-repeated lament that "RCIA just doesn't work" and the solution is to make it a more rigorous catechetical program.

After over twenty-five years of working in catechumenate ministry, there are two things I want to say when I think of these conversations. First, to those who feel they have failed, I say be gentle with yourself. This entire process is not up to us but is truly the Holy Spirit's work. It is not our job to guarantee conversion. Our proper role is to make our own lives of faith and conversion so visible and attractive to the seeker that they will want to enter into that way of faith and conversion in Christ themselves. To that end, let's remember that the only person we *can* change is us.

Second, to those who lament that the RCIA isn't working, I say that perhaps we simply have not done the RCIA as it was really intended. To borrow from G. K. Chesterton, the RCIA "has not been tried and found wanting." Perhaps, rather, "it has been found difficult; and left untried."

Shortly after the Latin text of the *Rite of Christian Initiation of Adults* was presented to the bishops of the world for translation into their various languages, Aidan Kavanagh, OSB, wrote a report to liturgical scholars and theologians outlining some of the major changes and challenges this new ritual would present to parishes around the world. He summarized the challenges of this new rite:

> Most clergy regard its implementation as problematic if not impossible. They are right. For what the Roman documents contain are not merely specific changes in liturgical rubrics, but a restored and unified vision of the Church. One might describe it as a concentric ecclesiology locked together by the sacramental discipline of faith shared on all levels . . .
>
> One may turn an altar around and leave *reform* at that. But one cannot set an adult catechumenate in motion without becoming necessarily involved with *renewal* in the ways a local church lives its faith from top to bottom. For members of an adult catechumenate must be secured through evangelization; they must be formed to maturity in ecclesial faith through catechesis both prior to baptism and after it; and there must be something to initiate them

into that will be correlative to the expectations built up in them through their whole initiatory process. This last means a community of lively faith in Jesus Christ dead, risen, and present actually among his People. In this area, when one change occurs, all changes. ("Christian Initiation in Post-Conciliar Catholicism," 7–8)

The Vision

If we approach the RCIA as yet one more program to implement and we delegate the implementation of that program to a small group of leaders, then we will have failed even before we begin. What Kavanagh pointed out back in 1977 was that the adult catechumenate changes everything. It is a paradigm shift that flows from the radical insight recovered from Vatican II that *baptism matters*. If that's true, then *your* baptism matters. It matters most of all to the people who are seeking what baptism gives you: an intimate relationship with the living Christ active in the world. Where we find that living Christ and that relationship is in the community of Christians.

Unfortunately, that community is messy. It is imperfect, made up of imperfect people. It would be much easier, cleaner, and quicker to just leave RCIA to a small group of highly qualified Christians who meet once a week to transmit the teaching of the church to a receptive, albeit passive, group of seekers. Or maybe we could ensure that the catechumens meet only the best of Catholics among us or attend only the best of our liturgies.

Yet the Body of Christ doesn't work that way. Only through intimate relationship with the members of Christ's Body will one touch and hear and see Christ at work in the world. So if you want your seekers to learn how to be the Body of Christ, they must be trained by those who are the Body of Christ: the entire Christian community.

The Reality

However, what happens most often in our parishes is that we make the RCIA an activity among many other parish activities. It is a small faith-sharing group among many other similar groups. To go through the RCIA essentially means to be part of this group. Operationally, we initiate people not into Christ, not even into the church, but into *this group* called RCIA.

Every so often, this RCIA group, like many of the other parish groups, will request to do some kind of ritual at Sunday Mass. And so we schedule it on the parish calendar along with the capital campaign announcement, the Mother's Day blessing, and the commissioning of new Communion ministers. Parishioners who would rather not be bothered will avoid the "RCIA Mass," and the unwitting ones who didn't read the bulletin will grumble that those RCIA people keep making the Mass longer.

Then for those who are "going through the RCIA," most of them have one goal in mind, and it's usually not lifelong discipleship. It's "graduation" when they will be done with RCIA classes and get their sacraments and their certificate. Then they can move on to whatever their real goal was, which was something like marrying their Catholic girlfriend, pleasing their grandmother, or getting the Catholic discount at the Catholic grade school. It's not really their fault they think this way because we told them that RCIA lasts from September to May and they only need to attend so many meetings with the RCIA group before their sacraments.

This is not the "unified vision of the Church" Kavanagh said changes everything. It's adult education for people who want to learn more about Catholicism. That kind of program is easy to implement, but it rarely changes the hearts of the catechumens, candidates, or parishioners. And if it does, it's because you had a special person like Rocio who took your program into her own hands.

Now there are indeed communities where the RCIA is thriving and the parishioners can't wait to celebrate the RCIA rites. Perhaps your community is one of these. I was lucky enough to be part of a community like this, and I thought we were doing what the RCIA called for. Yet, quite often in this community I heard a few longtime baptized Catholics say something that made my heart sink.

They saw the power of the catechumenate process. They felt their own hearts and lives change along with the catechumens. Then they lamented that they wish they had never been baptized as children so they could "go through the RCIA" as adults. This was the most distressing sign that what we were doing still was not what the RCIA envisioned.

Today, if I could speak to these adults who regretted being baptized as infants and to anyone who has said the same thing to you, I would say that you *are* going through the RCIA as adults. If you have adults preparing for baptism in your parish, you are doing RCIA, because the RCIA can't happen without you, the baptized community. The RCIA doesn't happen at a Wednesday night gathering, and it's not done by the RCIA team or the pastor. *All the baptized* are responsible for *doing* the RCIA because the catechumens in your parish are watching and imitating and learning from what *you* are doing as Christians each day, week after week. *That's* how they learn to become Catholic. You are their teachers; you are their models. So you are doing RCIA whether you know it or not.

Turning RCIA Upside Down

This book is an attempt to turn the way we do RCIA upside down, especially in how the community participates in this parish-changing, life-altering endeavor. If it's true that the entire community of the baptized is responsible for the initiation of adults, then we have to stop trying to get the community *involved in the RCIA* and instead get what we've been calling the RCIA *involved in the community*.

Instead of trying to help you convince parishioners to go to one more meeting or volunteer on another committee, I want to relieve you of that impossible task. Instead I want to give you practical ways to get your catechumens, candidates, and sponsors to be more involved in the life of the community where they will encounter the Body of Christ. And rather than show you how to create a curriculum for formation that you will have to implement,

I want to help you see the curriculum that is already within your community just waiting to be tapped that will move a seeker's heart closer to Christ. These shifts in thinking will make all the difference for seekers, your RCIA team, and your parish.

Now you might think doing this will require more of you. It will certainly require more of your commitment, patience, creativity, and vision. But it won't take more of your time or personal resources. In fact, it will be easier and less stressful because it won't depend all on you or on what your team alone can provide. You will find that you actually have way more time and resources than you originally thought. That's because you will be using what your parish is *already doing*, things that other people are already organizing, and tapping into those aspects of parish life to train catechumens and candidates in the Christian way of life.

By doing RCIA *this* way, you will not only be forming your catechumens and candidates. You will also be deepening the faith of your parishioners. You will be calling your community members to step up and take their rightful place as the baptized, "fully prepared in the pursuit of its apostolic vocation to give help to those who are searching for Christ" (*Rite of Christian Initiation of Adults*, 9).

Outline of the Book

In chapter 1, we'll lay the foundation for why your parish is the curriculum. That foundation is the church's understanding of the dignity and purpose of baptism. Then in chapter 2, we'll look at the community of the baptized and how they make up your RCIA team. We'll also describe some of the specific roles found in this great big team that is now made up of your entire parish. Chapter 3 will explore what your parishioners should be doing at various stages throughout the initiation process.

Chapters 4, 5, and 6 are the heart of the book, going deep into what an upside-down RCIA looks like. Chapter 4 surveys the comprehensive curriculum, already embedded in your parish, that the church gives for making disciples. Chapter 5 lays out the syllabus of the RCIA that your parish is already doing. We'll also analyze real-life parishes in the United States, of varying sizes and demographics, to see how their weekly activities can be used for discipleship formation. Next, in chapter 6, we answer the question everyone asks: When do you get to the *real* teaching? Here we show you *how* to teach your parish's RCIA syllabus more effectively using mystagogical catechesis.

We shift a bit in chapter 7 and examine the many different kinds of people in the RCIA, what syllabus is best for each of them, and how to know if the catechumens and candidates are "getting it." Finally, the conclusion is a reflection on what would happen if we transformed our initiation processes this way.

You're Not Alone

Sometimes, the hardest thing about doing RCIA ministry is feeling like you're on your own. I hope that after reading this book, you'll know that you're not. First, you'll have your entire parish community to lean upon and take some of the burden off of your shoulders.

Second, connecting people who do RCIA ministry with others who are passionate about the catechumenate is the very reason my husband, Nick, and I started TeamRCIA.com. There is so much I wanted to include in this book that just couldn't fit. So I hope you'll find your way there for more resources, to ask your own questions and find some answers, and to connect with other RCIA team members all around the world who share your love for the catechumens and candidates.

So let's get started on seeing our entire parish as the curriculum for making disciples.

Chapter 1

RCIA Isn't Just for Catechumens

Baptism Matters

Ask most ordinary Catholics what Vatican II did, and they might say it changed the Mass from Latin to the vernacular or it turned the priest around to face the people. These were certainly significant, but they are only outcomes of the real shifts that were so much bigger.

In the first document of Vatican II, the bishops expressed a foundational theological and ecclesial principle that, to some extent, had been forgotten over the centuries: Baptism matters.

The church has always taught this. But the shift in focus that Vatican II emphasized was to *why* baptism matters. Baptism matters because it changes us and gives us rights *and* duties:

> Mother Church earnestly desires that all the faithful should be led to that full, conscious, and active participation in liturgical celebrations which is demanded by the very nature of the liturgy, and to which the Christian people, "a chosen race, a royal priesthood, a holy nation, a redeemed people" (1 Pet. 2:9, 4-5) have a right and obligation by reason of their baptism. (Constitution on the Sacred Liturgy, 14)

For many Catholics in general, what had mattered most about baptism had been membership in the church because membership granted salvation. Heaven was opened to you because baptism washed away all sin. This is still the teaching of the church, but it is only part of our understanding of baptism.

More than just membership

Baptism is God's most beautiful and magnificent gift. . . . We call it gift, grace, anointing, enlightenment, garment of immortality, bath of rebirth, seal, and most precious gift. It is called *gift* because it is conferred on those who bring nothing of their own; *grace* since it is given even to the guilty; *Baptism* because sin is buried in the water; *anointing* for it is priestly and royal as are those who are anointed; *enlightenment* because it radiates light; *clothing* since it veils our shame; *bath* because it washes; and *seal* as it is our guard and the sign of God's Lordship. (Saint Gregory of Nazianzus)

Baptism changes *who* we are. It makes us sharers in Christ in whom we become priests, prophets, and kings. Because it changes *who* we are, it also changes *what* we do:

> From the fact of their union with Christ the head flows the laymen's right and duty to be apostles. Inserted as they are in the Mystical Body of Christ by baptism and strengthened by the power of the Holy Spirit in confirmation, it is by the Lord himself that they are assigned to the apostolate. If they are consecrated a kingly priesthood and a holy nation (cf. 1 Pet. 2:4-10), it is in order that they may in all their actions offer spiritual sacrifices and bear witness to Christ all the world over. (Decree on the Apostolate of Lay People, 3)

Thus, in all our actions as the baptized members of Christ, we offer our lives in thanksgiving to the Father and bear witness to Christ wherever we go. As royal priests, we lift up the needs of the world and ask God to transform them into a clearer image of the kingdom. As a holy people set apart as God's own, we establish right relationships with one another, with creation, and with God who created us. And as apostles, we are sent by the Spirit to be prophets, bearing the message of the Gospel: Look! Heaven is open. God is here. Come.

The Purpose of Baptism Is Mission

Baptism gives us work to do! It gives us a mission, one that will be challenging and inspiring. It will demand everything of us, perhaps even our very lives, but it also will give us a joy and peace like no other. It's a mission that changes the world because it changes people's hearts—from hearts filled with despair and darkness to hearts radiating enduring hope and joy. Although each one of us who is baptized is responsible for this mission, we never do this mission alone. We do it as an entire household of disciples who have been given all the gifts we need to accomplish it. Those gifts are baptism, which makes us members of the Body of Christ; confirmation that shapes us into the image of Christ; and the Eucharist, nourishing us with Christ's own Body and Blood.

> Thus the three sacraments of Christian initiation closely combine to bring us, the faithful of Christ, to his full stature and to enable us to carry out the mission of the entire people of God in the Church and in the world. (*Christian Initiation*, General Introduction, 2)

This is what we do when we prepare people like Rocio, whom we met in the introduction. We are training them for Christ's mission.

Once the focus of baptism shifts from membership in the church to mission in Christ, other things change too. We start to see baptism more like a verb than a noun. To be baptized is to respond by faith to God's initiative, for baptism is "above all, the sacrament of that faith by which, enlightened by the grace of the Holy Spirit, we respond to the Gospel of Christ" (*Christian Initiation*, General

Introduction, 3). We go from what could be a passive, defensive, or fearful way of living our faith (since our membership could lapse or be taken away) to one that is an active, joyful, and hopeful response to God's gracious gift.

If we see baptism this way, our life of faith becomes an ongoing, personal, and communal *becoming-into-baptism* as we grow more and more into the likeness of Christ. Baptism isn't the end of a process; it's just the beginning!

Living the Christian way of faith requires, then, a daily discernment of how God is calling us to respond by faith to our baptism. How am I responding to God's gift and living out the mission this gift gives me? How can we strengthen our faith as a response to God's call? And how do we teach others to respond by faith and take on the mission of Christ in the world?

We Learn by Doing, Especially by Praying

Vatican II gave us a way for learning how to live and deepen our faith so that we may respond as Christ did to his mission:

> In the restoration and promotion of the sacred liturgy the full and active participation by all the people is the aim to be considered before all else, *for it is the primary and indispensable source from which the faithful are to derive the true Christian spirit.* (Constitution on the Sacred Liturgy, 14, emphasis added)

Not a textbook or a program but rather our full, conscious, and active participation in the liturgy of the church is the primary and essential way we learn what it means to live as Christians. This is vitally important for RCIA teams. We should always remember that the *Rite of Christian Initiation of Adults* is just that—a *rite*. It's a liturgical process, not a catechetical program. Rather than being merely significant moments within a catechetical process, the rites themselves in the RCIA are the very means of forming new Christians. There are two implications to this key point.

Liturgy Draws Us into Life with God in Christ

First, liturgy is the principal place of formation because what we are introducing people to is not a doctrine but a person, the Person of Christ. Pope Francis emphasized this very point in his first encyclical, Light of Faith:

> Faith, in fact, needs a setting in which it can be witnessed to and communicated, a means which is suitable and proportionate to what is communicated. For transmitting a purely doctrinal content, an idea might suffice, or perhaps a book, or the repetition of a spoken message. But what is communicated in the Church, what is handed down in her living Tradition, is the new light born of an encounter with the true God, a light which touches us at the core of our being and engages our minds, wills and emotions, opening us to relationships lived in communion. (40)

Furthermore, this encounter with God in the liturgy goes beyond intellectual assent to touch our entire being—mind and heart, body and soul, human need, hope, memory, and feeling—so that we can have an intimate relationship with the living God:

> There is a special means for passing down this fullness, a means capable of engaging the entire person, body and spirit, interior life and relationships with others. It is the sacraments, celebrated in the Church's liturgy. The sacraments communicate an incarnate memory, linked to the times and places of our lives, linked to all our senses; in them the whole person is engaged as a member of a living subject and part of a network of communitarian relationships. (ibid.)

This new relationship gives us eyes of faith to see the world as God sees it, drawing us to live in the world with hope, joy, and profound love for everything and everyone God has created:

> While the sacraments are indeed sacraments of faith, it can also be said that faith itself possesses a sacramental structure. The awakening of faith is linked to the dawning of a new sacramental

sense in our lives as human beings and as Christians, in which
visible and material realities are seen to point beyond themselves
to the mystery of the eternal. (ibid.)

Those who are baptized participate Sunday after Sunday in the
eucharistic liturgy to be taught and shaped again and again by
Christ and to deepen their union with him through the breaking
of the bread.

Although catechumens cannot yet share in the Eucharist until
they are baptized, they are still called to participate fully, consciously, and actively in the liturgies of the church, especially the
Liturgy of the Word in the Sunday gathering of the parish, for
Christ is present there.

In the liturgy, little by little, over the course of the entire liturgical year, catechumens and candidates are being catechized by
Christ, who is present not only in the Eucharist, but also wherever
the faithful gather to sing and pray in his name. Christ is present
at the liturgy in the Scriptures proclaimed in the assembly, especially in the gospels. And Christ is present in the ministry of the
church, especially in the ministry of the priest (see Constitution
on the Sacred Liturgy, 7).

Catechesis Is for Living the Christian Life

If the RCIA is a liturgical process and the rites themselves are
the very means of forming new Christians, then what is the place
of catechesis in the catechumenate?

Obviously, liturgy is not the only thing the church does. However, it is "the summit toward which the activity of the Church is
directed; it is also the fount from which all her power flows" (Constitution on the Sacred Liturgy, 10). This gives us our second implication regarding Christian formation.

The church's ministries of evangelization and catechesis, its
communal and spiritual life, and its works of charity and service
all combine together to form a way of aiding and deepening the
Christian spirit derived from the liturgy so that we may live out

Christ's mission in the world. Everything we do leading up to the liturgy, and everything we do flowing from the liturgy, should strive to strengthen that primary encounter with Christ in the worshiping assembly.

Pope Francis invited us all to see catechesis in this way, as something bigger than merely teaching about the Christian faith. For the pope, catechesis is helping believers open their hearts to encounter the living Christ active in the church:

> The catechesis, as a component of the process of evangelization, needs to go beyond the simple realm of scholastics, in order to educate believers, beginning with children, *to encounter Christ, living and working in his Church*. It is the encounter with Him that gives rise to the desire to know him better and thus to follow Him to become his disciples. (plenary assembly address, May 29, 2015)

Therefore, evangelization to those who do not believe is meant to open their hearts to Christ, and catechesis for those who do believe prepares them to respond more faithfully to the Gospel of Christ, whom they encounter in the Christian assembly.

When Baptism Matters, the Parish Matters

The pope went on to ask this pointed question:

> The challenge for the new evangelization and for the catechesis, therefore, is played out precisely on this fundamental point: *how to encounter Jesus*, where is the most consistent place to find him and to follow him? (ibid.)

The most basic answer to that question is the Christian community doing what Christians do. Where we see that most clearly is in our parishes. In the parish, we actively work together to evangelize and catechize. Our communal life binds us closer together as we learn to follow the inspiration of the Holy Spirit and to sacrifice ourselves for one another. Our life of prayer nourishes us with the

Word and sacraments and strengthens us with God's blessings. And our apostolic life shown by words and works of mercy to the world make us credible witnesses of the Gospel.

Just as we learn the true Christian spirit through full, conscious, and active participation in the liturgy, we learn how to live and deepen that spirit by immersing ourselves into the whole of Christian life. We learn our faith by doing our faith with other Christians where they gather to pray, study, reflect, and serve.

In 1999, the US bishops wrote *Our Hearts Were Burning Within Us: A Pastoral Plan for Adult Faith Formation in the United States*. In a section titled "The Parish *Is* the Curriculum," they stated,

> Parishioners' personal involvement in ministry is also formative. They learn as they prepare for ministry and as they engage in it; they learn from those with whom they serve and from those whom they serve; and by their witness, they show others the life-giving power of faith. (119)

Here the bishops emphasized the hands-on nature of catechesis. We learn by doing; we learn by teaching and serving; and we learn by being models of faith for others. This will be the very way that parishioners, along with the catechumens and candidates, will deepen their own conversion and discipleship.

However, the bishops also expressed a caution that comes with understanding catechesis in this way:

> While this pastoral plan is concerned primarily with intentional adult faith formation programs, the success of such efforts rests very much on the quality and total fabric of parish life. This includes, for example, "the quality of the liturgies, the extent of shared decision making, the priorities in the parish budget, the degree of commitment to social justice, the quality of the other catechetical programs." (118, quoting *Sharing the Light of Faith: National Catechetical Directory for Catholics of the United States*, 189)

Forming Christian adults isn't an isolated activity that can be fulfilled simply through a discrete program labeled "adult faith formation" or "RCIA." The entire life of the parish influences and affects how adults are formed.

The RCIA process, like any other adult faith formation initiative, needs a parish of faithful disciples who make their parish a place of lively faith. Even the most amazing adult faith formation programs and processes, including the RCIA, will be ineffective if the rest of parish life falters. As RCIA teams, we cannot be concerned with only the catechumens and candidates. Our efforts in the RCIA involve not only them but the entire community of the faithful because it will be the parish that will help shape the faith of those seeking Christ.

- If there is a lack of unity, charity, and welcome among the people who gather for Sunday Mass, how will catechumens and candidates learn how to show that love to others in the world?

- If the quality of the liturgies demonstrates a lack of care for either the ritual or the assembly, how will catechumens and candidates learn to be a eucharistic people in their daily lives?

- If the homilies are lacking in hope, nourishment, or a call to respond in thanksgiving, how will catechumens and candidates learn to speak a word that will rouse the weary heart to come to know Christ?

- If the parish is lacking in the way it operates in its work practices, in the way it spends its money, and in its visible and tangible care for those in need in its neighborhood, how will catechumens and candidates be emboldened to proclaim the justice of God in the world even in the face of persecution or indifference?

To paraphrase another US bishops' document, *Music in Catholic Worship*, faith grows when it is well expressed in the parish community. Good parish life fosters and nourishes faith. Poor parish life may weaken and destroy it.

The Parish *Is* the Curriculum

The bishops' final statement in this section from *Our Hearts Were Burning Within Us* summarizes well this turn to the baptized and the entire life of the parish as the focus and milieu for adult faith formation:

> When these various elements of parish life are weak or lacking, formal programs for adults typically do not flourish; when they are vibrant and strong, they create an overall climate of active participation and living faith that can only benefit the parish's intentional formation efforts with adults. Thus, while the parish may *have* an adult faith formation program, it is no less true that the parish *is* an adult faith formation program. (121)

Because your parishioners have been washed, anointed, and clothed as priests, prophets, and kings, enlightened with the knowledge of Christ, endowed with the gifts of the Holy Spirit, and strengthened by the Eucharist to grow into the full stature of Christ for doing Christ's mission, they are the best teachers for your catechumens and candidates. Therefore, your parish is the best "classroom" for forming adults for living a life of discipleship in Christ.

Rethinking new evangelization

Sometimes an RCIA team member asks me how to get people who have fallen away from the church back. Often they aren't trying to solve a general ministry issue; they're praying that a loved one returns to faith.

When Pope John Paul II first wrote about new evangelization, he talked about "entire groups of the baptized [who] have lost a living sense of the faith, or even no longer consider themselves members of the Church, and live a life far removed from Christ and his Gospel" (On the Permanent Validity of the Church's Missionary Mandate, 33).

As painful as it is to see our loved ones lose faith, he said that announcing the Gospel to those who have never heard it must always be "the first task of the Church" (34). That task can never be diluted, secondary, or forgotten because of our concern for those whose faith has grown cold.

This is why Pope Francis's definition of "new evangelization" is important to remember:

> How many men and women, on the existential peripheries created by a consumerist, atheistic society, wait for our closeness and our solidarity! The Gospel is the message of the love of God who, in Jesus Christ, calls us to participate in his life. Therefore, this is new evangelization: to become conscious of the merciful love of the Father in order that we may become pure instruments of salvation for our brothers. (plenary assembly address, May 29, 2015)

We cannot change others' hearts; only the Holy Spirit can do that. We can only change ours. The best way we can persuade those who have left the church is to love them constantly but to love those who wait for our closeness even more. If, time and again, our absent loved ones see us working tirelessly to heal the wounds of those at the peripheries, that will be our greatest testimony that may, in the Spirit's time, inspire our loved ones to come home.

The Urgency of Our Mission

Any initiatives of the church that strengthen parish life, catechize Christians, or rekindle the flame of faith in Christians who have left must never be ends to themselves; they must always serve the primary mission of announcing the Good News to those who have never heard it, those like Rocio. People like her who seek something more for their lives have never been given a sense of hope or meaning that transforms and transcends the daily sufferings they bear. No one has invited them into a mission that changes their lives at their core and reveals the profound mystery that all human life is an image of the divine. There is no program, workshop, video, book, or course that will heal the wounds they bear. Only the living Body of Christ found in the Christian community, focused on the suffering of those at the peripheries, can do that.

Heal the wounds

The thing the church needs most today is the ability to heal wounds and to warm the hearts of the faithful; it needs nearness, proximity. I see the church as a field hospital after battle. It is useless to ask a seriously injured person if he has high cholesterol and about the level of his blood sugars! You have to heal his wounds. Then we can talk about everything else. Heal the wounds, heal the wounds. (Pope Francis, in Antonio Spadaro, "A Big Heart Open to God," *America*)

Rocio and people like her are waiting for us, the baptized, to show them the hope that is found in the love of God in Christ Jesus. They are waiting to hear that message of love, proclaimed by both word and deed by the Christian community: Jesus Christ has saved you. This is what Pope Francis called the "first proclamation." He named it "first" because "it is the principal proclamation, the one which we must hear again and again in different ways, the one which we must announce one way or another throughout the process of catechesis, at every level and moment" (Joy of the Gospel, 164).

If we are to announce this message "at every level and moment," we cannot limit our method of proclaiming it and teaching it to just a weekly meeting in a classroom, no matter how excellent that gathering may be. The only way that those like Rocio can truly hear and learn this first proclamation so that both their minds and hearts are opened to Christ is through the Christian community, living it out in their own daily lives, because that is where they will encounter Christ most fully:

- In the Christian community is where those who are first learning to respond to the Spirit's promptings practice hearing God's voice in the Scriptures and following the way of the Gospel.

- It is where they encounter Christ's abiding mercy in a community that regularly offers and asks for forgiveness of one another and joyfully sacrifices their own needs for the sake of the other.

- It is where they learn to readily turn to the Father in prayer and mark the daily moments of joy and grief with rituals that touch the heart.

- Most of all, it is where they learn to walk with those in need, offer their friendship, and give reason for their hope.

In turn, the best way for us, the Christian community, to deepen our own grasp of the fundamental teaching that Jesus Christ has saved us and to draw those who have lost their connection to that message is to go out and show that saving love to those who wait for the Gospel that liberates.

In the next chapter, we'll look at who makes up the Christian community that is the place of encounter with Christ, and we'll explore the specific roles of the parish assembly in their responsibility for training adults in Christ's mission.

Chapter 2

Your Team Is Bigger Than You Think

How Getting People to Sing Taught Me about RCIA

"The initiation of catechumens is a gradual process that takes place within the community of the faithful" (RCIA 4). Most of us have probably read that statement from the *Rite of Christian Initiation of Adults* and believed we understood what it meant. I thought I did when I first started leading the RCIA team in my community back in the early nineties. Many years later, I realized I didn't get the full implications of that simple sentence.

I was a music director for many years. One of the biggest problems every music director faces is trying to get an assembly to sing. Just before Mass each Sunday, standing there with the choir in front of the church, I would ask the assembly, "Please join us in singing the opening song." The opening song is one of the most important parts of the Mass for the people to sing, so I always made sure to choose a song the assembly knew. Then I'd turn around to face the choir and direct them. Every so often during the song, I'd look behind me to check in on the assembly. Those sitting in the front of the church were singing pretty well, and I felt great. I had done my job getting the assembly to sing!

When I was no longer serving in music ministry, I sat in the pews with the rest of the assembly. There I began to see a bigger picture. One Sunday, I sat in the middle pews of the church. Before Mass started, the new music director made the same plea to the assembly: "Please join us in singing the opening song," and then she turned her attention back to the choir. I did what I was trained to do and opened the hymnal and began to sing. From where I stood, I could hear the choir pretty well, and I also heard those in the front pews joining in. But the singing wasn't as strong among the people around me, and I heard nothing from the people in the pews behind me. I figured it was just a fluke, and maybe with a more familiar song, the singing would be better.

The next week, I arrived at Mass late, so I sat toward the back of the church. I had made it just in time to catch the last few verses of the opening song, "Amazing Grace." I knew the song by heart and started singing. But no one around me in those back pews even had a hymnal open, and most of them were just standing there not even trying to sing. The choir sounded great, however— the new microphones they had installed really picked up their voices and the sound filled the church. And yet, no one around me was singing, although they seemed to enjoy listening to the choir.

Then one Sunday in July, there was no choir, just the music director. She had given the choir the month off and invited the choir members to be at Mass and sit with their families wherever they wanted to in the pews that month. Before Mass began, the music director greeted the assembly and explained that the choir was taking a break this month but that they were still here sitting in various places throughout the church.

"So for all of July," she said to us, "the choir for Mass is you, the entire assembly!" The people laughed, and she made the typical invitation for all of us to sing, but she said it this way: "Okay, choir, let's sing together!"

I was sitting near the back of the church, and I noticed that several people around me actually opened up the hymnal. The song began. It was "On Eagle's Wings." We all sounded a bit tentative with that opening verse. But once we got to that soaring refrain, the people found their voice, even the ones sitting in the very back of the church! It was like you couldn't keep us from singing. The sound resonated off the walls and filled that space like no other, and it wasn't because of any microphone system. It was simply the assembly realizing and hearing for themselves that no one else was going to do the singing, so *they* would. This revelation must have unlocked something in them because when it came time for the Communion song, they really took over. The music director was also the pianist that day. So when it was time for her to go to Communion toward the end of the song (another classic, "I Am the Bread of Life"), she decided just to let the assembly sing *a cappella*, without accompaniment, while she received Communion. Well, I thought the roof was going to blow off that place when we got to that highest note in the refrain. It was stunning, and I think it even surprised some of those sitting with me in the back rows how powerful they all sounded together.

What was going on here? It couldn't be that the assembly simply decided that day they would sing. Here's what I think happened.

First, the "experts," the choir members, weren't secluded to one side of the church to sing *for* the assembly. They were mixed in throughout, supporting the people from within.

Second, the invitation to sing wasn't "join *us*," that is, the professionals, in this song we're going to sing for you. Rather, it was "together, let's sing." There were no experts, and there was no audience listening to the experts. There was only us, singing together songs we knew and loved. Some of us sounded better than others, and they encouraged and supported the ones who were more uncertain. At that *a cappella* moment during Communion, when all the sound was coming only from the voices of the people, it was absolutely clear that "[t]he entire worshiping assembly exercises a ministry of music" (*Liturgical Music Today*, 63) and that "unrehearsed community singing . . . is the primary song of the Liturgy" (*Sing to the Lord*, 28).

We weren't perfect or polished by any means, but we were all in it together. And not just the people in the front who always sang, but even the squirmy kids in the back and their frazzled parents trying to herd them. Even the ones who didn't come to Mass every week but came when they could. They were humming along and every so often made an attempt to sing a phrase or two. At whatever level of ability each had, all of us were giving what we could to those songs because now the task of singing them was *ours*.

Does RCIA Happen in Front of or Within the Community?

As leaders, it can be very easy to have a bit of tunnel vision that limits our perspective. We don't intentionally do this, and most times we're not even aware of it. It's simply human nature to see the world from one's own standpoint and assume that everyone else sees the world the same way.

According to a Center for Applied Research in the Apostolate (CARA) Catholic poll from 2012, only 2.8 percent of the entire United States Catholic adult population considered themselves very involved in their parish outside of Mass. These are the less than three people for every one hundred people in your parish who serve as the staff, leaders, ministers, and volunteers of your entire parish. These are the people you'll usually see at Mass sitting up front or serving in a liturgical ministry. They know all the other 2.8 percent by name and form an enthusiastic and close-knit group in your parish. They're the ones who are at Mass every Sunday, go to parish meetings during the week, and arrive early and stay late.

In most parishes, the work of forming catechumens and candidates in the life of faith has been delegated to the "experts," the RCIA team, who are part of your parish's 2.8 percent. And every week, the RCIA coordinator dutifully invites the rest of the community, your 97.2 percent, to "join in." She updates the community on what the RCIA team is doing and encourages the rest of the parish to show concern for the catechumens and candidates by joining in on the work of the RCIA team. Her invitations are heartfelt and gracious, and some people respond. They become sponsors; some give a presentation at the RCIA meetings; others commit to praying. Coordinators of parish groups come in to the RCIA meeting to talk about their ministry. And whenever there's an RCIA rite at Mass, everyone seems to be involved—at least from what you can see.

This all works to some extent. Your most engaged parishioners—your 2.8 percent—will likely also be very invested in the formation of these catechumens and candidates. They'll be the first to volunteer to be sponsors and presenters and whatever else you need for RCIA. And it will look like the RCIA is taking place "within the community of the faithful" because you have all these people participating in the work of the RCIA.

As members of the 2.8 percent, our perspective of what happens in our parish often comes from our standpoint of being "in front" and on the inside. This is not the perspective of the other 97.2 percent. As much as we might want to think otherwise, many of the people in our pews do not always get what we're trying to do with the RCIA. And certainly the vast majority of them would never say that they are doing anything with the RCIA, much less having any responsibility for the initiation of adults.

But that's exactly what the church expects. Here is what one of the documents from Vatican II says specifically of the people's role in the catechumenate:

> This Christian initiation, which takes place during the catechumenate, should not be left entirely to the priests and catechists, but should be the concern of the whole Christian community, especially of the sponsors, so that from the beginning the catechumens will feel that they belong to the people of God. (Decree on the Missionary Activity of the Church, 14)

Catechumens and candidates don't "join the RCIA." They are joining Christ, and the only way to be joined to Christ is to belong to the people of God. So the people of God, not the RCIA team, are doing the RCIA.

Building on that statement from Vatican II, the *Rite of Christian Initiation of Adults* says this about the people's responsibility:

> [T]he people of God, as represented by the local Church, should understand and show by their concern that the initiation of adults is the responsibility of all the baptized. Therefore the community must always be fully prepared in the pursuit of its apostolic vocation to give help to those who are searching for Christ. In the various circumstances of daily life, even as in the apostolate, all the followers of Christ have the obligation of spreading the faith according to their abilities. (RCIA 9)

"Responsibility," "obligation"—those words communicate more than "join us." They imply that the RCIA is a duty for us all; the RCIA team is here to only help the people of God fulfill that responsibility.

Another implication found here is that the *way* the people do their responsibility is not extraordinary. That is, it does not typically require them to do something above and beyond what they should already be doing as members of the apostolate, the baptized faithful. They, in fact, are to show their concern and exercise their responsibility for the catechumens and candidates by doing the ordinary things they are already doing as Christians. Your parishioners don't need to go to another meeting or join another committee. They're already swamped with everything else in their lives! Instead, your RCIA team's job is to help your parishioners recognize that everything they are already doing, in the parish and in their daily lives as Christians, affects what the catechumens and candidates are learning about the Christian way of life.

When your parishioners start to get this, a couple of things will happen with them. First, they will become much more attentive to how they are living as Christians, especially when catechumens and candidates are around. Are they modeling Christian teaching in their own behavior and attitudes? Are they being good examples of discipleship in their homes, workplaces, neighborhoods, as well as the parish? Are they actively participating in the liturgy and parish life? Do they speak readily about their own faith, especially to people in need, and work to ease the suffering of those around them?

Second, your parishioners will begin to understand that RCIA isn't a group. It's more like being family and what families do to welcome in and teach new members how to be part of the family.

Jake

I have a two-year-old nephew named Jake. He's the only child of my only sibling, and I don't have children of my own, so Jake gets a lot of attention from my family. I first met Jake when he was three days old. My husband, Nick, and I each held him in our arms, and he felt like a little rag doll, completely dependent and fragile. But as he grew older and started learning how to interact with people, we could tell by the look on his face or things he pointed to that he was learning . . . all the time.

Nick and I love visiting Jake and hearing from his parents all the new things Jake has learned since our last visit. My brother said that Jake had learned how to turn on the TV and which button to push to start the coffeemaker, all before he turned one! It hadn't been their intention to teach him those things; Jake just learned by watching.

I had my own experience with this during one of my visits. I had been checking my emails on my phone, and Jake suddenly grabbed it. After he dutifully tried to chew one corner of it, he held it in one hand, and without hesitation used his finger to push the "on" button. He knew exactly what to do just from watching me . . . except for the chewing part. He must have learned that from someone else!

Catechumens and candidates pick up on how to live as Christians even if we're not intentionally teaching them. Like Jake, they will watch and imitate and learn how to be disciples from what we do in their presence.

Becoming Family in the Household of God

Almost every catechumenate team I talk with wants the parish to be more involved with the RCIA process. When I ask them why, however, their answers get a little fuzzy. Sometimes their answers focus on the practical. They need more sponsors, more catechists, more help on the team. Other answers focus on the benefit to the parishioners. They would learn so much or they would get so much out of it. And some answers focus on the benefits to the catechumens and candidates. They would learn more about what we do as a parish and how the parish works.

All of these are great reasons for involving the parish in the RCIA process, but I don't think they get at the heart of the matter. Ask yourself, what is the number-one purpose of the entire initiation process? The answer is in the very first sentence of the RCIA. The rite of Christian initiation is a process for those who are seeking the living God and who wish to "enter the way of faith and conversion" (RCIA 1).

Loving Jesus Means Loving Jesus's Family

Now let's translate that into a real-life experience. One day, you meet the love of your life, and you want to become part of this person's life, including his or her family. But this person comes from a completely different country than you do and you don't know anything about the culture and customs. How are you going to make this work? What is the best way to "enter the way" of his or her family?

My husband, Nick, grew up in a white, middle-class, suburban neighborhood in the Midwestern United States. He has three siblings, but they all live pretty far from one another and from their parents. So his family holidays at his parents' house are usually small, quiet gatherings with everyone sitting around the table. There are the traditional dishes: turkey for Thanksgiving, ham for Christmas, mashed potatoes and gravy all around, and pumpkin or apple pie for dessert. If there's music, it comes from a radio playing softly in the background. After dinner, they sit in the living room and read or chat. It's a peaceful and lovely evening.

Now I grew up in an urban, Filipino family in Los Angeles. I only have one sibling, but most of my aunts, uncles, cousins, and second cousins live within the same county. Some of us even live blocks apart from each other. For us, a small family gathering has at least twelve people. For our usual holiday gatherings, we have forty to sixty people coming and going throughout the day and evening. We never have a table big enough to fit everyone around it, so our meals are always buffet-style, with enough food to feed a village. Our holiday menus include the typical turkey and ham, but also a couple of noodle dishes, adobo, and several whole fishes, some kind of Filipino stew, plus fried chicken someone brought, and Filipino-style bread rolls. Don't forget the row of gallon-sized cookers serving up heaps of rice for everyone. For dessert, in addition to pie and ice cream, we have a kind of sticky rice wrapped up in banana leaves and a coconut and gelatin concoction that looks like stained glass. And talk about loud! The conversations are a mishmash of Taglish (English and Tagalog combined) yelled from across the rooms. And if we aren't all talking (at the same time!), then we are all singing loudly around the piano or the karaoke machine. My family parties are definitely not the place for people who need peace and quiet.

When we were first dating and because he loves me, Nick wanted to learn more about my Filipino culture. He likes to cook, so he found some recipes for traditional Filipino dishes and tried a few out on me. I even taught him some Filipino words and told him stories of what I remember growing up in my family. All of this helped him feel closer to me. But it wasn't until he started hanging out with my family that he started to feel (and be treated) like a member of the family.

The first time I brought Nick to one of my family's big Filipino gatherings, it was a bit of culture shock for him. No matter how much I tried to prepare him for the day, he really just had to experience it for himself to get a sense of what it was like to be part of my family. It was the same for me the first time I spent the holidays with his family. The only way we were going to really be part of each other's families was to put ourselves where they were and to do the things they did. It was the only way either of us was going to learn how to be a member of the family in more than name or association.

You become a member of any family by hanging out with them—all of them, not just a handpicked few. You learn how to act like family by spending time with them, in formal and informal situations, and by letting them hang out with you. It's the same for those who want to become members of Jesus's family. Only by having the catechumens and candidates become part of the life of the parish—and having the parishioners become part of theirs—will they "enter the way of faith and conversion."

Parishes, Like Families, Are Not Perfect

Now my family is pretty amazing. But like every family, mine has members with their own eccentricities, foibles, and even sinfulness too. There's always the one who drinks just a little too much, the one who can say the most hurtful things without even knowing it, the one who doesn't talk to anyone, and the one person you just never agree with on anything. As a family, we have our shortcomings too. We don't always say things out loud that need to be said, and boy, can we hold a grudge. Because we can be so tight-knit, it's not always easy for outsiders to feel a part of the group. And did I mention how loud we are?

I bet your parish is a lot like my family. You love them all, but there are those extra special members of God's household who aren't always the best representatives of the Christian way of life. They might complain about everything and never have a nice thing to say to anyone. Or maybe they aren't so good at participating at Sunday Mass, or they just don't seem to care very much about anything beyond themselves. Maybe as a whole, your parish could do better in some areas of discipleship. Our parishes, like our families, aren't perfect. So how will we ever get the catechumens and candidates to "enter the way of faith and conversion" by involving them with this ragtag bunch of barely involved Catholics?

Well, here's the thing. Your parish is the Body of Christ. It is not going to be the Body of Christ someday. There isn't some ideal Body of Christ's community you can go visit with your catechumens and candidates. The Holy Spirit led them to you and to your parish. You can't give them back, and you can't ask for an extension until your parish improves.

As flawed as I think my family can often be, I know that the first time I brought Nick to meet them, they worked hard to welcome him and help him feel at home. Many of them made sure to engage him in conversations, and when they found out he liked to cook, several of them shared their own cooking secrets. One of my aunts had made sure to have some "American" food on the table, but they all encouraged him to try out some of the less familiar items too. Nick tried it all, except for one dish that was just beyond his comfort zone, but no one pushed. When the conversations got really passionate and the Tagalog words were flying fast and furious, someone remembered Nick was there and they translated for him. Those who felt more comfortable speaking English took the lead in chatting one-on-one with Nick. Those who were less confident about their English skills still made sure to thank him when it was time to leave.

Just like my family, I am certain that our parishes do the same when they are aware that they have guests and newcomers in their midst. Or at least, that's what we'd work toward, because it's simply what families and parishes do when someone new wants to be part of them.

Welcoming seekers into "the way of faith and conversion" is the most important thing we do. Think about it. If a family had a great sense of community but never welcomed new people into it, slowly, one-by-one, the family would die off. If a parish did the same, we'd have the same fate. But the reason we need to get the community involved in welcoming seekers goes deeper than self-preservation. It's why parishes exist. The Trinity is the ultimate community of love, but it's not a closed system. God is constantly drawing all creation into that community of love. It's the reason God became one of us, and it's the reason we exist as Christians. Integrating the catechumens and candidates into that Christian community of love is the biggest, most essential mission that the Holy Spirit has set before our parishes.

This may seem daunting. But if my family can do it, then so can our parishes.

Team Members Within Your Community

Just like your family, everyone is part of it, but not everyone has the same role. The RCIA team that is your entire parish works the same way. Everyone is responsible, but each person plays a different role in that shared responsibility for the initiation of new members into Christ. Here are some specific roles within your RCIA team.

The People of God

This is the most important team member because without them, you can't introduce seekers to Christ. Your parishioners, individually and as a body, have the responsibility of constantly being the face of Christ to everyone they meet. You can find a summary of their responsibilities in paragraph 9 of the RCIA, and we'll look more closely at these in chapter 3.

Although the entire parish is your team, you wouldn't invite the entire parish to an RCIA team meeting. But you would certainly find every possible opportunity to get your catechumens and candidates meeting and hanging out with parishioners whenever and wherever parishioners get together.

You might think you already do this. But here's a real example of how I completely overlooked this important RCIA team member.

Our parish was about to welcome our new pastor the following Sunday. The bishop would be there for a special Mass to bless the pastor, and after Mass, the entire parish was invited to a meal and fiesta in the parish hall. I was pretty excited because that same Mass was also when we would dismiss our catechumens. So I knew that our bishop and our new pastor would get to meet our catechumens briefly during Mass.

Our practice every Sunday for dismissal was to have a team member go with the catechumens to break open the Word for about half an hour. Then for about another hour, we'd do a little bit of catechesis, and that was the RCIA gathering for the week.

So here I was with our catechumens that Sunday in a small classroom in the parish hall. We had just finished our dismissal reflection on the Sunday readings, and I heard the people from Mass starting to gather in the hall for the fiesta with our new pastor. As we started with the catechetical part of our gathering, I was trying to keep our catechumens' attention on the lesson I prepared on whatever the topic was for that week. But all we could focus on was the music and laughter coming from the hall and the smell of the food wafting in through the doorway. After a while of trying, it finally dawned on me! What was I doing keeping these people here in this classroom trying to teach them how to be part of God's family when God's family was right outside having a grand time being family together?

So I told our catechumens that our catechesis would be to go to the parish fiesta in the hall. We packed up, and I took them out to the feast. I introduced them to the bishop, who got to talk with them for a good while. None of the catechumens had ever met a bishop before, and they were touched by his generosity toward them. They also chatted with our pastor and the president of the parish council. The catechumens didn't know that parishes had councils or that you didn't have to be a priest or nun to be part of it. While standing in line for food, I introduced the catechumens to Betty, who was serving plates of enchiladas. Betty was also the head of our parish food pantry. The catechumens got a personal invitation from Betty to come help any Friday to make sandwiches for the homeless in our neighborhood. Then we sat down at a table with Cathy, a single mom raising a young daughter. Cathy and one of our catechumens who was also a single mom really hit it off, and they became good friends from that day forward.

The catechumens later told me they had an amazing time meeting so many people from the parish and they learned so much about what the parish does. They were so excited to continue learning about their new Christian family. The people of God gave a much better lesson to our catechumens than anything I could have prepared that day.

You can help your parishioners exercise their role in the initiation of adults by constantly looking for ways to put the catechumens and candidates in touch with them, individually and in small groups. Make these encounters the primary way you form seekers in the Christian life, and think of your own separate RCIA gatherings as supplemental and secondary. We'll go much deeper into this topic in chapter 5.

The Domestic Church

Within the people of God, there is another sacred space where formation happens, and that is the Christian home. The domestic church is a microcosm of the parish church in that the members of that household practice the disciplines of Christian life in very direct ways with one another, their neighbors, their fellow citizens, classmates, and coworkers. In the Christian home, there should be a practice of reflection on the word of God, prayer, sacrificial life, and service, just as in the parish church. Find ways to connect catechumens and candidates to Christian households to help them learn how to make their own homes a place where faith lives. One idea called "dinner ministry" is described in chapter 3 on page 51.

Baptized Candidates

We hardly ever think of the baptized candidates—those preparing to be received into the full communion of the Catholic Church or those preparing for confirmation and Eucharist—to be members of our RCIA team. Aren't they the focus of what the RCIA team does?

In many ways, they are. But because of the dignity of their baptism, the primary role of the baptized candidates is the same as that of the people of God. Even if they are as new to living out the Christian way of life as your catechumens, their baptism gives them the right and duty to pray *for* the catechumens and to support them by their own deepening of their life of faith in Christ.

Whenever you have prayers, blessings, or rites specifically for the catechumens, be sure the baptized candidates are there within the assembly praying along with the people of God.

The Bishop

For most of us, the diocesan bishop (or archbishop) is not a member of our parish. Yet, the bishop serves a very important role in the church's work of initiation. The bishop is a symbol of the universal Catholic Church and its unity. In the work of initiation, he has several responsibilities. We find these described in various places throughout the RCIA but especially at paragraph 12. Some of these are the following:

- Show care and concern for catechumens by reminding all the baptized that their first priority is to evangelize.

- Delegate qualified catechists to lead the catechumenate in parishes.

- Act as the primary catechist of the diocese.

- Preside at the Rite of Election, listen to the testimony of godparents, and elect the catechumens for initiation.

- Moderate the period of mystagogy primarily through his preaching during the Sundays of Easter, and gather with the neophytes near Pentecost.

Most of us will never work with a bishop, but here are some simple ways you can help your bishop exercise his role in initiation:

1. Take advantage of times during the year when the bishop might be at your parish, and bring your catechumens, candi-

dates, sponsors, and neophytes to meet the bishop at those parish gatherings.

2. Invite your catechumens and candidates to write brief letters to your bishop sharing their faith journey and how God has been active in their life and asking the bishop to pray for them. Do this early from the beginning of their formation, not just near the Rite of Election.

3. During the period of mystagogy, write a note to your bishop asking him to remember the neophytes on each of the Sundays of Easter.

The Priest or Pastor and RCIA Director and Deacon

The RCIA makes no mention of an RCIA director or even a team. However, RCIA 13 and 14 does talk about the priest and his responsibilities, and RCIA 15 mentions how permanent deacons assist in whatever way is needed. In most parishes, the pastor would typically delegate many of these responsibilities to others on staff or to coordinators and volunteers in the RCIA. So these responsibilities could also be shared with an RCIA director, deacon, or other coordinators:

- Instruct catechumens and candidates in the Christian faith by apprenticing them in the living word of God, community life, prayer, and works of mercy (see RCIA 75).

- Call the entire parish to be models and examples of living the Christian way of life.

- Care for the rites of the catechumenate by working with the parish liturgist and music director; if there is no liturgist or music director, then work closely with presiders and liturgical ministers to be fully prepared for the rites.

- Provide pastoral care to catechumens and candidates through not only spiritual guidance but also genuine attention to their personal needs and calling the entire parish to do the same,

especially by selecting good sponsors for each catechumen
and candidate.

- Assist the catechumens in discerning and choosing good godparents, and approving their choice of godparents.

Here are some ways to help your priest, pastor, RCIA director, or
deacon fulfill their responsibilities:

1. Go beyond asking your priest, director, or deacon to "teach a
   class" for the catechumens and candidates because that's only
   one part of catechesis. Invite them also to pray for and with
   the catechumens and candidates, to have spiritual conversations with them, and to just hang out or do works of service
   with them.

2. Prepare your presiders well in advance of each RCIA rite. So
   they may preach well during the rite, help them get to know
   the needs of your catechumens and candidates.

Ambassador of Welcome (Inquiry or Precatechumenate Coordinator)

This is a role that you won't find anywhere in the RCIA, but
it's helpful to have at least one person attending to the tasks of
this role. If you go to almost any hotel, restaurant, store, or con-
vention center, there is always someone there whose main job is
to greet and welcome you and to answer any questions you might
have. They are constantly looking for the visitors and newcomers
and are always happy to serve in whatever way is needed.

As Christians, we go beyond a customer-service kind of welcome.
We give a spiritual welcome, a welcome into Christ. It's not merely
a job we do; it's an attitude we constantly have. Your "ambassador
of welcome" is someone who has this attitude and more. Here are
some things they would do beyond your average church greeter:

- Be present at places where there would be visitors and newcomers, such as Easter, Christmas, wedding, baptisms, and
funerals.

- Interact with people in places outside of your parish to be a face of Christ and a person who naturally invites others to meet Christ in the parish.

- Be always on the move, not just standing at a table or at the doors of the church, but actively looking for new faces and starting conversations with them.

- Connect inquirers directly with a person on the RCIA team in a timely manner, and follow up with the inquirer to make sure they have connected with an actual person who will help them get started in their journey.

Persons who serve in a similar kind of way are your parish receptionist, secretary, bulletin editor, and website coordinator. They should always perform their duties with the needs of the newcomer and inquirer in mind.

Sponsor Coordinator

While an ambassador of welcome is focused on the newcomer, a sponsor coordinator concentrates on the parishioners. The RCIA itself doesn't mention a sponsor coordinator, but especially for parishes with many catechumens and candidates, having a dedicated person responsible for attending to the needs of sponsors and godparents can be helpful.

- Know the community and the personalities, skills, and experiences of many individuals and families in the community, always looking toward "matchmaking" them with current and future inquirers and candidates.

- Invite and recruit potential sponsors year-round, making sure there is someone ready from the community at any given time of the year.

- Pair up people long before the Rite of Acceptance or the Rite of Welcoming.

- Work with inquirers if they ask to bring their own sponsors.

- Support, encourage, nurture, and train sponsors in their role, helping them understand how to be good companions (for more information on the role of sponsors, see chapter 6).

- Ensure sponsors know the schedule of rites, and assist in rehearsing sponsors for these rituals.

Catechist

When you think of RCIA ministries, this is typically the first person you think of. The RCIA briefly describes the catechist's role in paragraph 16; however, the catechist's primary responsibility is to see the big picture of how each catechumen and candidate is being formed through the entire work of the parish:

- Provide catechesis that is suitable, gradual, and complete in its coverage (RCIA 75.1).

- Ensure that formation is systematic by going beyond traditional classroom teaching and including formation in all four areas of discipleship found in RCIA 75.

- Use the objectives in paragraph 75 and the markers of readiness in paragraph 120 to discern how well each catechumen and candidate is living the four areas of Christian discipleship.

- Put people in touch and intimate communion with Christ through the community's encounter with the mystery of Christ revealed throughout the entire liturgical year.

- Discern and attend to the unique formation needs of each catechumen and candidate.

- Be aware of the local customs and activities of the community, such as special feast days, traditions, and events that can be part of formation for initiation.

Together, Let's Sing!

In his apostolic exhortation The Joy of the Gospel Pope Francis reminds us of the essential authority and responsibility that each member of the faithful has:

> In virtue of their baptism, all the members of the People of God have become missionary disciples (cf. *Mt* 28:19). All the baptized, whatever their position in the Church or their level of instruction in the faith, are agents of evangelization, and it would be insufficient to envisage a plan of evangelization to be carried out by professionals while the rest of the faithful would simply be passive recipients. (120)

No one among the baptized is a spectator when it comes to the initiation of adults. All of the baptized—regardless of how catechized or poorly catechized they are—have a rightful place among the faithful who together teach a new song to those seeking Christ. They don't need much training, just an invitation to give what they have in the work of our shared mission in Christ. Again, Pope Francis says,

> Every Christian is challenged, here and now, to be actively engaged in evangelization; indeed, anyone who has truly experienced God's saving love does not need much time or lengthy training to go out and proclaim that love. Every Christian is a missionary to the extent that he or she has encountered the love of God in Christ Jesus: we no longer say that we are "disciples" and "missionaries," but rather that we are always "missionary disciples." If we are not convinced, let us look at those first disciples, who, immediately after encountering the gaze of Jesus, went forth to proclaim him joyfully: "We have found the Messiah!" (*Jn* 1:41). The Samaritan woman became a missionary immediately after speaking with Jesus and many Samaritans come to believe in him "because of the woman's testimony" (*Jn* 4:39). So too, Saint Paul, after his encounter with Jesus Christ, "immediately proclaimed Jesus" (*Acts* 9:20; cf. 22:6-21). So what are we waiting for? (Joy of the Gospel, 120)

What *are* we waiting for? Those seeking Christ need all of us now to take on our baptismal mission. We who lead the church's work of initiation have a profound opportunity to encourage all the faithful in its mission and mandate and to renew entire communities with the love of Christ.

In the next chapter, we will look specifically at how the faithful fulfill their responsibility to initiate adults within the various stages and significant moments of the RCIA.

Chapter 3

Five Things Parishioners Do in the RCIA

What are we asking parishioners to do, exactly, when we ask them to be more involved in the initiation process?

The purpose of the *Rite of Christian Initiation of Adults* is to lead seekers on the way of faith and conversion (RCIA 1). It is important that the parish as a whole serve as a guide to the seekers because the parish is our best example of the way of faith and conversion.

So what we are asking parishioners to do is to be a shining, clear example of a people of faith and a community of conversion. While this is somewhat easy to grasp, it can be very difficult to pull off. People are fallible. We are often unfaithful. We often resist change. RCIA team members exhibit those failings themselves, and they witness those failings in their fellow parishioners. So, without really even thinking about it, we tend to shield the seekers from the larger parish community and focus on the "RCIA community."

But in reality, there is no RCIA community. The seekers are not joining the RCIA. They are joining Christ. And the place they find

Christ is within the Body of Christ—the body of believers that we call "parish." That is the only community that can initiate the seekers into the way of faith and conversion.

"Hence, the entire community," says the RCIA, "must help the candidates and the catechumens throughout the process of initiation . . . " (9).

If we take this seriously, then our job as RCIA leaders shifts a little bit. When I first started, I thought my job was to help the seekers, catechumens, and candidates. But in actuality, our job as RCIA team members is to coach the parish so that they, the Body of Christ, can help our seekers, catechumens, and candidates.

The RCIA lists five stages along the way of faith when the community actively takes on this initiating role. The tasks the community has in each stage are described at paragraph 9 in the RCIA.

Before we look at the first part of the RCIA in which parishioners participate, let's review how we evangelize.

Three Levels of Evangelization

The RCIA presumes that seekers come to us somewhat evangelized. However, we know that there are millions of people in the world who have never heard the good news that God loves them. As Christians, we are obligated to go out into the world— beyond the walls of the church—to share that good news.

In Pope Paul VI's apostolic exhortation On Evangelization in the Modern World he described three levels of evangelization:

- Wordless witness

- Explicit witness

- Community witness

Many of us are pretty good at the first level, wordless witness. This is simply living out our faith in ways that might seem contrary to the general culture. We are caring, forgiving, understanding, and hopeful even when those around us are not.

The second level is harder for many of us, but just as important. Pope Paul said that when we live as Christians should, our behavior will cause others to ask questions of us. We have to be ready to be able to make an unambiguous proclamation of the reason for our hope, which is Jesus. Without this overt declaration of Christ as our reason for living this way, evangelization does not happen (see On Evangelization, 22).

The third level of evangelization—community witness—is where the RCIA proper begins. This level is described in paragraph 9.1 of the RCIA. We'll look at that more closely below.

All three levels of evangelization are necessary for genuine faith to be grounded in the heart of the seekers. Our work as RCIA teams is not limited to the third level, although that is the level we most often recognize as the "beginning" of the RCIA. However, each of us must do our part to exercise the first two levels of evangelization in our own lives. Furthermore, when seekers come to us asking for initiation, we must discern if they are truly evangelized. The purpose of this initial stage is to discover in the seekers what their wounds are and if they have some glimmer of Jesus's promise of healing love for them. (For more information on a process for this initial discernment, see Nick Wagner's *Seek the Living God: Five RCIA Inquiry Questions for Making Disciples*.)

Dinner ministry

One challenge RCIA teams often have is we are not always ready when seekers come to us. We wind up telling them to come back in a few months when RCIA begins. But what if we could have something immediately available this week, planned around their schedule and availability that did more than put them into a group meeting with other seekers, that you don't have to lead?

One simple idea you can implement right away is a "dinner ministry." Ask three or four members of the parish if they would be willing to host dinner in their homes once or twice every year for people who want to begin the process for becoming Catholic. All they have to do is provide a meal, home-cooked or take-out, and welcome a seeker and a companion from the parish into their homes for that meal. There is no agenda to the gathering other than getting to know one another and helping the seeker feel welcomed and connected to some members of the parish.

You might give the dinner hosts a few conversation starter questions, but usually you just have to encourage them to share their own stories. After the first few dinner ministry meals, you will see an effect on both the seekers and the people who volunteer to host the dinners. The hosts will feel enriched by the conversations, and the seekers will make some lasting connections with people in the parish.

Period of Evangelization and Precatechumenate (RCIA 9.1)

In this period the church reminds us of the "supreme purpose" of all the members of the faithful: "that Christ's message is made known to the world by word and deed and that his grace is communicated" (9.1). This sounds pretty straightforward. However, the way the church envisions all of us doing this might surprise us:

- Give evidence of the spirit of the Christian community.

- Welcome seekers into homes.

- Welcome seekers into personal conversations.

- Welcome seekers into community gatherings.

Notice that none of these tasks requires any significant training on the part of the parishioners. They simply have to offer their guests basic hospitality. This is the essence of what the RCIA is asking parishioners to do in the precatechumenate stage—offer genuine hospitality to the seekers. This job is ongoing and constant. There's no start date or end date for it. Thus there's no "beginning" to the period of the precatechumenate, and there's no schedule of classes for it. Every day of the year is when the parish community participates "in the RCIA" by being attentive to seekers in their midst, whether it's those they meet in their daily lives or at the parish Sunday gathering.

What is one thing your team can do this year to coach the parish toward accomplishing its supreme purpose? See the "Dinner ministry" sidebar for one simple idea.

Celebrations Belonging to the Period of the Catechumenate (RCIA 9.2)

Once a seeker has entered into the order of catechumens through the Rite of Acceptance, he or she begins "an extended period . . . [of] pastoral formation and guidance, aimed at training them in the Christian life" (RCIA 75). (Baptized candidates cannot become catechumens since they are already baptized. However, if they do not yet know how to live as Christians, they may participate in some elements of the training the catechumens receive [see National Statutes for the Catechumenate, 31].)

Unfortunately, too often, we think of this formation process as a small-group gathering to explain doctrine. The RCIA says we must provide a "suitable catechesis" for the catechumens and candidates. However, catechesis is much more than acquainting them with dogmas and precepts. Catechesis is an encounter with Christ. Remember that Pope John Paul II said,

> the definitive aim of catechesis is to put people not only in touch but in communion, in intimacy, with Jesus Christ: only He can lead us to the love of the Father in the Spirit and make us share in the life of the Holy Trinity. (On Catechesis in Our Time, 5)

The purpose of the catechumenate is to train the seeker in the Christian life. Our fullest expression of Christian life is our intimate encounter with Christ when believers gather to worship. That's why the RCIA says the parishioners have to show up for all of the rites belonging to the catechumenate and "take an active part in the responses, prayers, singing, and acclamations" (RCIA 9.2). If the catechumens and candidates encounter a Spirit-filled, joyful community that is worshiping God at full tilt, that will teach them about the way of faith and lead them to communion and intimacy with Jesus Christ.

Preparing the Assembly for the Rite of Acceptance

The Rite of Acceptance into the Order of Catechumens is a complex rite. If it is not done well, it can rightly cause parishioners to complain that it adds too much time to the liturgy. A poorly executed rite also diminishes the ritual experience of encounter the seekers have with Jesus. Therefore, we have to prepare the ritual prudently, making full and intelligent use of the options to omit, include, choose, and adapt various parts of the ritual as allowed by the rubrics and introductory notes, all in light of the particular circumstances of your community and those celebrating the rite.

We also have to prepare the assembly well. There are two aspects to preparing the assembly for a rite: a practical aspect and a spiritual aspect.

Practical Preparation

Under the practical aspect, let's make sure there is good communication with the community, letting them know several weeks ahead of time when the rite will take place. You can also provide a bit of catechesis regarding the purpose of the rite, the primary symbols of the rite, and who the subjects of the rite are, that is, the seekers who are becoming catechumens. You can do this through the parish bulletin and website, in brief announcements during Mass or before it, and in the homilies leading up to the rite. (For a ready-to-print bulletin insert you can download to help your assembly prepare for the Rite of Acceptance, go to TeamRCIA.com/ypitc.)

Other ways to make sure the parish community is ready for the rite is to communicate with various groups of the parish. For example, instead of simply asking the choir to prepare music for the Rite of Acceptance, let them know a little bit more about the rite itself and the people celebrating it. Give them some reasons why the rite is important and how their participation in it will strengthen the new catechumens and their sponsors. More importantly, help them see how the rite might deepen their own faith.

Do this with other parish groups, such as the liturgical ministers, the schoolchildren and their parents, the parish council, the youth group, and the small faith-sharing groups. Make sure to give them all the names of those who will be celebrating the rite and their sponsors and invite them to pray for them by name.

Spiritual Preparation

Spiritual preparation is less about giving the community information about the rite and more about forming them for the rite.

First, create a spiritual preparation question—a kind of "question of the week"—that individuals, families, and parish groups can use as a reflection question during the weeks leading up to the rite. This spiritual preparation question can be connected to the readings that will be used for the rite, one of the prayers or questions asked during the rite, or the purpose of the rite itself.

For example, imagine that your upcoming Rite of Acceptance will be taking place on the Second Sunday in Ordinary Time, Year B, when the gospel reading comes from the first chapter of John. In that gospel reading, John the Baptist points to Jesus and says, "Behold, the Lamb of God." Then two disciples of John go to follow Jesus, who says to them, "What are you looking for?"

A few spiritual preparation questions for the Rite of Acceptance based on this gospel reading might be,

- In your life right now, what are you looking for from Jesus?

- Is there something missing in your heart right now? How might Jesus fill your need?

- Where do you find Jesus?

- How can you be like John the Baptist and help others find and follow Jesus?

Invite your parishioners to reflect on these questions during the weeks before the Rite of Acceptance. Ask your parishioners to hold their responses in their hearts and call them to mind as they prepare to celebrate the Rite of Acceptance with your seekers. Then at the rite itself, integrate these questions (and your own responses) into the homily or into the commentary or welcome that takes place before Mass.

There are other rituals that happen during the catechumenate, such as liturgies of the word specifically for the catechumens, blessings, anointings, and minor exorcisms. Although these other rites often take place in smaller gatherings during the week, the community should nonetheless be invited to take part in them as much as possible, preparing for them practically and spiritually. Many of these other rituals can also take place during the parish's weekday Masses or at the weekly meetings of your parish groups, in addition to your usual RCIA gatherings during the week.

Turning the Hearts of the Assembly

One rubric at the beginning of the Rite of Acceptance is that a group of the faithful goes out of the church with the ministers to meet the candidates for the rite and their sponsors (see RCIA 48). I strongly encourage you to invite the entire assembly to go outside to greet the candidates and to celebrate the first part of the Rite of Acceptance outside the church space. Yet, I know that for most assemblies, this is an unusual invitation, and many may be reluctant to get out of their seats to do this.

I was assisting in a parish where we wanted to invite the entire assembly to go outside for the Rite of Acceptance, which would take place in several weeks. Jeff, our inquirer, had been coming to our parish for several months already and had been very moved by the passion for works of charity and justice that the parish showed in its many activities with the homeless and immigrants in our neighborhood.

Before each Mass I had an opportunity to make a brief announcement to help prepare the assembly for the Mass. Four weeks before the Rite of Acceptance, I stood in front of the assembly before Mass and I told them about Jeff:

> Many of you might have already met Jeff or seen him here in our parish gatherings. He'd like to one day be baptized. He told me the other day that he has been so touched by the way that you care for those in need in our community. And he wanted me to let you know that he wants to care for others like you do. He and his sponsor, with all of us, will be celebrating a ritual called the Rite of Acceptance in just a few weeks at this Mass. This is the first step for him toward baptism. I'd like to ask you to pray for Jeff in these coming weeks so that he can learn well how to love others like Jesus loved us.

The next week, I told the assembly another story about Jeff:

> Last week, I told you that Jeff was so touched by how this parish cares for those in need. This week, Jeff told me that he saw how you all welcome visitors and newcomers in our community. He said it's not just a handshake, but you have really shown genuine care for him and others like him through your conversations and by spending time with him after Mass. He is so eager to become baptized and to begin that formation in a few weeks. So please keep praying for him.

The following week, we had another story about Jeff and invited the assembly again to keep praying, letting them know that the following week would be the Rite of Acceptance at that Mass.

The day of the rite came. The RCIA team and the priest were anxious. What if no one wanted to go outside to greet Jeff for the Rite of Acceptance? What if they didn't understand what we were doing in the rite? I was a little worried too, but I trusted in the goodness of our parish. And a little extra prayer beforehand didn't hurt either.

Before Mass, I stood before the assembly for the usual announcement. But I knew nothing was going to be usual today:

> I've been telling you all about Jeff these last few weeks. You know how much his heart has been touched by your Christian witness, by your love for one another, and your care for those in need. You know how much he wants to be just like us and to follow Jesus with us. And I know you've all been praying for him these last several weeks so that he can open his heart to Christ. Well, Jeff is waiting outside right now with his sponsor. He is waiting and hoping that we will help him find and follow Christ. Please, let us go and welcome him. Let us go and pray for him and bring him into the church so that he can learn to hear and follow Jesus.

We started singing a song we all knew by heart, and the ministers who had been standing in the sanctuary began walking down the aisle, following the cross bearer toward the church doors. And the RCIA team and liturgical ministers got up and began inviting the assembly to follow the ministers and the cross outside.

To our great surprise, almost everyone immediately got up and followed us out the doors into the small open space between the church and the parking lot. There, Jeff and his sponsor were waiting. The assembly, with the help of the ushers whom we had trained beforehand, began surrounding them, forming a circle of song around them. Even many of our older parishioners were right there as fellow assembly members made sure they had a steady arm to lean on if they needed it.

That day was a turning point for our parish because it was the day their hearts turned to Christ found in Jeff our seeker. That day it felt like the rite really mattered to them. They weren't just being present at a rite because it was scheduled at the Mass they happened to be at. They had prepared themselves for the rite, with only a few stories and an invitation to pray. They felt invested in making sure Jeff was welcomed well and began his formation supported by the community.

This kind of preparation of the assembly isn't difficult, but it takes more commitment, planning, and patience. What you're doing here isn't just involving the parish in the rites of the RCIA. What you're really doing is helping them build a relationship with your seekers. Like any kind of relationship-building, that is a gradual process and requires a bit of vulnerability on everyone's part. But the reward is so much more than you can imagine or plan for.

Rite of Election (RCIA 9.3)

The period of the catechumenate ends on the day of the Rite of Election, which usually takes place on or near the First Sunday of Lent. This rite begins the next period of growth and formation called the period of purification and enlightenment. Most parishioners will never participate in the Rite of Election because it is held at the cathedral or another central church, and space is limited. However, the RCIA says, "The election, marked with a rite of such solemnity, is the focal point of the Church's concern for the catechumens" (121). Therefore, this rite should be the total focus of attention for the parish community from the moment seekers enter the catechumenate. This is because at this rite, the catechumens are given a promise by the bishop. The bishop promises that they will be "initiated into the sacred mysteries at the next Easter Vigil" (RCIA 133). This promise is irrevocable, and the Rite of Election is a no-turning-back moment. All the effort your parish makes on behalf of the catechumens is to bring them to this key conversion moment.

Yet, if most parishioners cannot participate in the actual Rite of Election, how will they be able to demonstrate their concern for the catechumens at this crucial moment?

The RCIA tells us, "The faithful, when called upon, should be sure to give honest and carefully considered testimony about the catechumens" (9.3). Testimony is an interesting word. It literally means "witness." It shares that meaning with the word "martyr"—someone who is a witness to faith. The most important thing that the members of the faithful can do to support the catechumens along the way of faith is to testify—give witness—to the faith of the catechumens. It will require some self-sacrifice (a small martyrdom) on their part to involve themselves significantly enough in the lives of the catechumens so that, when called upon, they can give their testimony.

The RCIA team can help the faithful prepare to fulfill their duty to give testimony about the catechumens by providing many opportunities for the faithful to interact with the catechumens throughout the period of the catechumenate. We will explore various ways this can happen in chapters 4 and 5.

When it's time for the faithful to give testimony, the relationship they have built with the catechumens will allow them to give "honest and carefully considered testimony" for the Rite of Election. (The faithful may also give testimony on behalf of the baptized candidates throughout their formation, especially if they will celebrate the optional Rite of Calling the Candidates to Continuing Conversion.) However, providing the entire community an opportunity to give testimony will require some creativity on the part of the RCIA team to come up with ways to call upon the faithful to do so without trying to do it all within the rite. See the sidebar for some ideas. (Also go to the following website for a ready-to-print bulletin insert you can download to help your assembly prepare for the Rite of Election: TeamRCIA.com/ypitc.)

---

20 ways to involve the parish in the day of election

1. Before Lent begins, invite parishioners to write a letter to the pastor about a catechumen preparing to be elected. The testimony about the catechumen should have God as the subject of the sentence. For example, "God has done this in Jeff's life: God has moved Jeff to serve God's people by praying for those in need among us and his presence at our parish gatherings." This way, the testimony doesn't become a tribute

to the person's good works but is rather a statement of praise for God's initiative and work in the catechumen's life.

2. Invite parishioners to write a letter to the bishop about a catechumen. The testimony about the catechumen should have God as the subject. See idea #1.

3. Place a box or basket for each catechumen in the gathering space or vestibule of the church. Provide parishioners with 3" x 5" cards on which they can write testimonies for the catechumens to place in their box or basket.

4. Create a private email address where parishioners can send messages testifying about a catechumen. Each testimony should describe God's action and work in the catechumen's life.

5. Ask the confirmation candidates to write a testimony for a catechumen.

6. Ask the children of the parish, especially the First Communion candidates, to draw pictures of the catechumens and how they have seen God acting in each catechumen's life. If they don't know the catechumens (why not?), have them draw a picture of how they hope God will act in the catechumens' lives.

7. Collect all the written and emailed testimonies and the drawings into a parish archive.

8. Encourage sponsors to keep a journal that tracks the times they have seen God act in the life of their catechumens.

9. If the godparents are different people than the sponsors, encourage them to do the same.

10. Encourage spouses and other family members to do the same.

11. Encourage the rest of the team to do the same.

12. Schedule a retreat day well before the Rite of Election to discern who will be chosen for baptism. Make testimonies part of the retreat experience.

13. Invite parishioners who cannot attend the retreat to fast and pray for those who will be discerning.

14. Write your own testimony for each catechumen, and give it to him or her on fine stationery.

15. Invite the elderly and homebound of the parish to pray for those who will testify about the catechumens.

16. Invite the neophytes (those baptized at the last Easter Vigil) to pray for the catechumens and those who will testify for them.

17. In the weeks before the Rite of Election, provide a "question of the week" for parish households to reflect upon based on the journey of the catechumens. For example, "How have we seen God's Spirit active in the catechumens?"

18. The week before the Rite of Election, publish a description of what testimony is and isn't.

19. During the optional parish rite of sending, invite the assembly to testify for the catechumens. Have a wireless microphone available to hear people's testimonies.

20. In the optional parish rite of sending, sing an acclamation at the conclusion of the testimonies. Choose an acclamation everyone knows well.

Lent and the Period of Purification and Enlightenment (RCIA 9.4)

In one way, this is the easiest point along the way of faith for the faithful to show their support of the elect because Lent is already filled with many opportunities to pray for and with the elect. (Although you may have baptized candidates at this time also preparing for sacraments, the primary focus of this period is the elect. Baptized candidates deepen their own conversion by joining with the faithful in being present at the rites for the elect and being examples of renewal for them.) Here, the primary role of the faithful is twofold.

Be Present at the Scrutinies and Presentations

First, the faithful "should take care to participate in the rites of the scrutinies and presentations" (RCIA 9.4). The scrutinies normally take place at the Masses of the Third, Fourth, and Fifth Sundays of Lent. In these simple rites, the faithful pray intensely for the elect during the silent prayer over the elect, in the intercessions that are specifically for the elect, and in the exorcism prayers over the elect that ask God to release their hearts from anything that is sinful and strengthen all that is good.

In addition to the three scrutinies, there are two presentations celebrated with the elect. First is the Presentation of the Creed during the third week of Lent. Here, the faithful hand on this treasure of the church to the elect by ritually proclaiming to them the words of the Creed. The elect, in turn, receive the Creed by listening intently to the proclamation of these words spoken to them by the faithful. Be sure to follow this rubric of the presentation (see RCIA 160) and not reduce the Creed to a piece of paper given to the elect. In the church's wisdom, we hand on our faith by the words we say and by our presence. This oral tradition reflects the Creator's sacred act of speaking the world into being and connects our action to Christ who is the Word made flesh among us. The aural tradition of hearing God's word and responding to it by our lives reminds us that we should be "doers of the word and not hearers only" (Jas 1:22).

The Presentation of the Lord's Prayer during the fifth week of Lent incorporates the same principles. In this rite, the deacon or priest proclaims the Gospel in which Jesus teaches his disciples to pray. Through this proclamation, the elect receive the Lord's Prayer.

Be Examples of Renewal

The second way the faithful participate in the elect's preparation for initiation is by giving "the elect the example of their own renewal in the spirit of penance, faith, and charity" (RCIA 9.4). In other words, the faithful should do Lent really, really well. This means that the elect should see the faithful participating in the three disciplines of Lent: prayer, fasting, and almsgiving.

In addition, if your parish has special Lenten celebrations and gatherings for the parish, such as reconciliation services, Stations of the Cross, soup suppers, or ministry to those in need, be sure to have your elect, catechumens, and candidates, along with their sponsors and godparents, also participating in these events and activities. Although it may be nice to schedule similar gatherings just for the RCIA group during Lent, it is better that they join *with* the parish in the community's usual Lenten practices of prayer, fasting, and works of charity. In this way, you enable the faithful to perform their primary duty of being examples of the spirit of penance, faith, and charity.

At reconciliation services where the sacrament of penance is also celebrated, you will want to ensure that your catechumens, elect, and candidates participate in the appropriate manner. Those who are unbaptized cannot yet celebrate the sacrament of penance, but they can certainly be present to pray not only for themselves but also for those who will celebrate reconciliation. Your baptized candidates should be prepared and encouraged to celebrate reconciliation as part of their preparation for Reception into the Full Communion of the Catholic Church or for the celebration of confirmation and Eucharist. Be sure their sponsors and godparents also serve as witnesses of conversion and renewal by participating in these special Lenten prayers and events.

The elect should also see and learn from the faithful how to live a penitential lifestyle. In addition to the usual Lenten celebrations of reconciliation, we can exercise daily disciplines throughout the year that shape our vision for always seeking repentance and a spirit of conversion. Pope John Paul II described what this penitential lifestyle looks like in his apostolic exhortation Reconciliation and Penance: "It is one's whole existence that becomes penitential, that is to say, directed toward a continuous striving for what is better" (4).

Penance isn't something you do once in a while; it's a lifestyle and an orientation that guides our attitudes and actions. The *Catechism of the Catholic Church* gives us ways to practice this lifestyle so that we can continuously strive for what is better. See the sidebar for this list.

How to live a penitential life

The *Catechism of the Catholic Church* gives us examples of daily disciplines for striving for what is better. Here are descriptions from the Catechism of the many forms of penance in Christian life:

1435   Conversion is accomplished in daily life by gestures of reconciliation, concern for the poor, the exercise and defense of justice and right [cf. Amos 5:24; Isa 1:17], by the admission of faults to one's brethren, fraternal correction, revision of life, examination of conscience, spiritual direction, acceptance of suffering, endurance of persecution for the sake of righteousness. Taking up one's cross each day and following Jesus is the surest way of penance.

1436   Daily conversion and penance find their source and nourishment in the Eucharist, for in it is made present the sacrifice of Christ which has reconciled us with God. Through the Eucharist those who live from the life of Christ are fed and strengthened. "It is a remedy to free us from our daily faults and to preserve us from mortal sins" [Council of Trent (1551): DS 1638].

> 1437   Reading Sacred Scripture, praying the Liturgy of the
> Hours and the Our Father—every sincere act of worship or
> devotion revives the spirit of conversion and repentance
> within us and contributes to the forgiveness of our sins.

Period after Baptism (RCIA 9.5)

Often, the period after baptism is misunderstood as a time to sign up the neophytes (the newly baptized) for ministries in the parish or to offer more classroom experiences. However, if you've waited until now to get your newly initiated involved in the ministries of the parish, then you've waited too long.

I don't mean that you should be signing up your catechumens and candidates to be lectors or Communion ministers during their catechumenate! It does mean that participation in the ministries of the parish takes on many forms, not just liturgical, and your neophytes should be participating in the ministries of your parish even as catechumens. For example, they can certainly participate in a variety of parish groups, such as Bible study, prayer groups, and service ministries to those in need. But their primary liturgical role during the catechumenate is to focus on being nourished by the word of God and the prayer of the church.

As neophytes, they will do what all the faithful are called to. The RCIA says that the period of postbaptismal catechesis or mystagogy is "a time for the community and the neophytes together to grow in deepening their grasp of the paschal mystery and in making it part of their lives" (244). The faithful here are called to continue being examples of a sacrificial way of life—a life that is shaped by the Gospel and the cross, since both are, in essence, one and the same. Recall back to the Rite of Acceptance where the seeker was asked if he or she was ready to follow "the way of faith along which Christ will lead you in love toward eternal life" (RCIA 52A). Their acceptance of this path immediately led them to be marked by the "sign of [Christ's] love" (RCIA 55A), the sign of the cross, the symbol of death and resurrection in Christ. Therefore, at this final period of the initiation process, we come full circle to continue to be people immersed in this paschal mystery.

To do this, the RCIA gives the faithful and the neophytes four specific ways that they are to deepen their grasp of the paschal mystery:

1. The *community* of the faithful and the neophytes

2. Meditate on the *Gospel*

3. Share in the *Eucharist*

4. Do the works of *charity* (see RCIA 244)

Notice that these are the same areas of formation listed in RCIA 75 that are used for training catechumens and candidates in the Christian way of life during the period of the catechumenate. The only specific difference is that now the Eucharist and the sacraments give the neophytes a new lens for perceiving their faith, the church, and the world (see RCIA 245).

Therefore, everything that the faithful did to help form the catechumens and candidates should continue in this period for the neophytes. In addition, everything the people of God did to welcome seekers at the very beginning of the initiation process during the period of evangelization and precatechumenate also should be done with even more charity for their new Christian sisters and brothers. Specifically, the faithful should "welcome the neophytes with open arms in charity, and help them to feel more at home in the community of the baptized" (RCIA 9.5).

Finally, the neophytes and their godparents, as well as all the faithful, "should take part in the Masses for neophytes, that is, the Sunday Masses of the Easter season" (RCIA 9.5). This is because the main setting for mystagogy is the Masses on the Sundays of the Easter season (see RCIA 247). Mystagogy isn't a separate event outside of Sunday Mass. It's not another RCIA class or gathering during the week. Mystagogy *is* the Sunday Mass because *Christ* is the mystagogue—the one who reveals the mystery—and there is no better or fuller place to encounter Christ than when the people of God gather to celebrate the Eucharist on the Lord's Day. It is not the catechist, nor the priest, nor the RCIA director who teaches the neophytes about the mystery of Christ but Christ himself who reveals himself to us:

> The Risen One, in the power of the Holy Spirit, is the mystagogue who opens our minds to understand the liturgy. . . . The revelation of the mystery of God is always an act of God, because only the mystery reveals the mystery. Just as every time that the church breaks the bread of the Word it is Christ himself who is the exegete of his mystery contained in the Scriptures, so when the church as mystagogue initiates Christians into the mystery contained in the liturgical action, it is Christ himself who opens their minds to understand the liturgy. (Goffredo Boselli, *The Spiritual Meaning of the Liturgy,* 9–10)

These Sundays are the first times your neophytes will encounter the fullness of the Risen One in the Liturgy of the Eucharist since they had been dismissed from the Mass during their catechumenate. So make sure that the faithful participate in these Sunday Masses of the Easter season with as much enthusiasm and care as they do for the Sunday Masses of Lent and the liturgies of the Triduum. In fact, we have been promising the catechumens all along that they will experience the joys of heaven at the banquet of the Lord, so we should make sure that these Sundays are the best Masses of the entire year!

What the faithful have to do to become more involved in the initiation process is not especially difficult. However, the discipline of keeping the seekers at the forefront of the parish's concern will be an ongoing challenge. People are busy and easily distracted. Our constant task as RCIA teams is to be continuously and creatively encouraging and coaching the faithful to take up their role in helping the seekers to enter the way of faith and conversion. In chapter 5, we'll go even deeper into specific ways parishes do this. But for now, in chapter 4 let's take a look at the curriculum for making disciples and how your parish life is the place where that training happens.

Chapter 4

The Curriculum for Making Disciples

How Did Jesus Train His Disciples?

In chapter 3, we looked at what the *Rite of Christian Initiation of Adults* asks the community of the faithful to do. In this chapter, we shift our focus to what is asked of the catechumens and candidates, and we will examine what the RCIA envisions as the curriculum for those who want to live the Christian way of life.

When we hear the word "curriculum" we automatically tend to think of classrooms, books, and exams that prove we know the material, or at least that we can give the right answers on the test.

However, the way Jesus trained his own disciples was not in a classroom but on the road, in people's homes at the dinner table, near the sickbed, in the temple, at a wedding, by the graveside, and on the sea where his followers worked for a living. Wherever people were curious enough to wonder about why Jesus lived that way, doing what he did, he invited them to follow. Then he took them out and lived the way he wanted them to live, and they learned by his side. After a while, he sent them out two by two on their own and told them to heal the sick and preach the kingdom. They returned and told him what they saw, and he broke open their experience for them, helping them understand its meaning for their lives. At the end of his own life, he said to his companions, "I have given you a model to follow, so that as I have done for you, you should also do" (John 13:15).

Jesus's last mandate to his own disciples was "Go, therefore, and make disciples of all nations . . . " (Matt 28:19). Our mission, then, as Christians who follow Christ's way of life, is to make disciples, who will make disciples, who will make disciples. Our curriculum for making disciples should look like Jesus's own course of study. Furthermore, it should help seekers *live* and not just *know about* his teachings and way of life.

Just after he announced that the church would celebrate an extraordinary jubilee year of mercy, Pope Francis said this to his Vatican council for promoting new evangelization:

> [T]he question of *how we are educating in faith* is not rhetorical, it is essential. The response calls for courage, creativity and the decision to take paths which are at times yet unchartered. (plenary assembly address, May 29, 2015)

How can we be creative and courageous in our catechesis, going beyond intellectual understanding of the faith to helping seekers encounter Christ alive and present in the church? The very answer to that is to look at what our parishes do week by week. First let's look at the content of this curriculum for making disciples.

What's the List of Topics for RCIA?

"Where can I find the text for teaching RCIA?" "What's the schedule of topics we should use with catechumens and candidates?"

Whenever someone asks me these questions, I feel a bit like I'm entering that story in the Bible with Jesus and the young rich man. In the end, I'm guessing one of us will be walking away disappointed.

I certainly have a list I can give you. You'll see the topics are pretty comprehensive, systematic, and substantial. Any catechumen or candidate—even any of us!—who goes through this material and learns everything on it will be strengthened in their faith, will know the foundational teachings of the church, and will be equipped to live a life of discipleship. It's the best curriculum I could find for teaching catechumens and candidates because it's the curriculum the church gives us for this task.

Still, it's probably not the kind of list those who ask these questions are looking for. But if you really want to teach your catechumens and candidates what they need to know to follow Jesus, then read on.

The Church's Training Course for Making Disciples

The list of things you need to teach catechumens and candidates is described in the RCIA at paragraph 75. Let's start with what the first part of that paragraph says:

> The catechumenate is an extended period during which the candidates are given suitable pastoral formation and guidance, aimed at training them in the Christian life.

Two definitions of "candidates"

Don't get tripped up by the word "candidates" in the RCIA text and think the rite is talking about baptized candidates. "Candidate" has two definitions in the RCIA. One refers to a person's baptismal status, indicating he or she is baptized. The other refers to a person's ritual status, meaning he or she is the focus of a particular rite, as is a confirmation candidate or an ordination candidate. "Candidates" here in RCIA 75 refers to the people who are the focus for baptism.

The catechesis that unbaptized adults and some baptized candidates need is a *training* in Christian life. (See RCIA 400 and chapter 7 for why the RCIA is not for all baptized candidates.) In the original Latin text of the RCIA, the word for training is *exercentur*, indicating that the catechumens "exercise" the disciplines of Christian life.

Okay, confession time. When I'm traveling, I often stay up late and surf the channels on the hotel TV. Sure enough, I'll end up watching one of those half-hour-long infomercials. You know the ones that promise you a beach-ready body if you buy their video program. Well, I have two of those video programs, still in their original boxes, sitting by my bed. Every morning, those boxes remind me that if I want a beach-ready body, I have to do more than just have the videos. I even have to do more than just open up the box, pop in the DVD, and watch them as I sit on my couch. I have to actually get up and *do* the exercises in the video. More than that, I have to do them every day!

Are Your Catechumens and Candidates Disciple-Ready?

The church basically says the exact same thing about training catechumens and candidates, but without the annoying sales pitch. My friends who train for marathons and Ironman Triathlons are out exercising every day. They follow a strict diet and sleep schedule. They research the best running shoes, work on their flexibility to avoid injury, and practice mental exercises to help them prepare for the long miles and steep climbs. They do some reading and study, too, about running, but they'd never make it through a race without the actual, daily physical training.

Now unlike discipleship training, many of my friends who run train mostly on their own. Some join running groups or have a training partner, but for the most part, they can train for a race by themselves. Sometimes, we might treat training in the RCIA in the same way and give catechumens or candidates a list of things to do, a set of videos to watch, or a book or two to read on their own. Once they've completed those things, we say they're good to go. However, discipleship training doesn't work that way.

If you go to your RCIA text and look up that first sentence of paragraph 75 we quoted above, you'll find a footnote at the end of it. That footnote refers you back to paragraph 14 in a document from Vatican II called the Decree on the Missionary Activity of the Church:

> Those who have received from God the gift of faith in Christ, through the Church, should be admitted with liturgical rites to the catechumenate which is not a mere exposition of dogmatic truths and norms of morality, but a period of formation in the whole Christian life, an apprenticeship of sufficient duration, during which the disciples will be joined to Christ their teacher.

Not only do we have here a clear description of what RCIA is not—"mere exposition of dogmatic truths and norms"—but we also have an even stronger depiction of what the training program of the RCIA is: an apprenticeship.

Apprentices don't just learn a trade; they enter a community of skilled professionals. Apprentices need a teacher, one who has mastered the skills. They also need a guild or union, some kind of community of people skilled in that trade. The community helps to measure an apprentice's level of competency in the various areas of that craft. They also provide an environment where the apprentice learns not only *how to do* the work but also *how to be recognized* as a member of that guild, that is, take on its culture and lifestyle.

One might be able to receive information about the Christian life through lectures, presentations, or catechetical books, but a catechumen—a person new to the Christian faith—or a candidate weak in the practice of one's faith cannot learn how to actually live the Christian life that way. They learn the Christian life by hands-on doing of the things Christians do.

Furthermore, an apprenticeship in Christian life "should be long enough—several years if necessary—for the conversion and faith of the catechumen to become strong" (RCIA 76). It's going to take time. I'd really like to be able to put on a bathing suit next week to show off my beach-ready body because I binge-watched all the videos in the program and did all the exercises three times every day this week. But muscles don't work like that. Neither does conversion, faith, and discipleship. Christian disciples, like muscles, need practice, exercise, and time to grow strong.

If you're eager to help your catechumens and candidates become disciple-ready in the whole of Christian life through this apprenticeship process that promises long-lasting results, then let's turn off the DVD, put away the textbook, get out of the classroom, and, as Pope Francis says, smell like the sheep.

The Curriculum for Discipleship Training

Here is the curriculum the church gives us at RCIA 75 for making disciples. The areas of training are broken down into four main disciplines: word, community, worship, and witness.

RCIA 75.1: Training in the Area of Word

This first area of training is typically what we think of when we think of catechesis, that is, a presentation of teachings and precepts. So we put together our syllabus, our schedule of lessons, and gather up our slides, videos, and handouts. And we're good to go!

But be careful. That's exactly what the church says is not a complete catechesis. That's because catechumens or candidates need to be led "not only to an appropriate acquaintance with dogmas and precepts but also to a profound sense of the mystery of salvation in which they desire to participate" (RCIA 75.1).

"Mystery," "desire"—you can't hand these out like facts. They require hanging out with and breathing the same air as the company of other Christians who live their faith with a sense of that mystery of salvation. Remember Rocio in our introduction? For her to develop a sense of the mystery of the living Word and a desire for living out the dogmas and precepts of that Word, she needed us to communicate to her *why* our faith mattered and made a difference in our lives. Developing that sense of mystery and longing also calls for falling in love with the Scriptures and making it a daily part of a catechumen's or candidate's contemplation on Christ.

Lastly, you can't cram for this kind of knowledge and attitude. It has to be "gradual and complete in its coverage, accommodated to the liturgical year, and solidly supported by celebrations of the word" (75.1). Only by meeting Christ every Sunday of the entire liturgical year, and meeting his friends—the saints who have gone before us and the holy people of God who make up your parish—will the catechumens and candidates receive a complete and systematic training in this area of the Word.

Faith-sharing skills for your team

Part of being Word people is seeing our life and faith *through* the lens of the living Word. We don't just *study* the Bible as one might analyze a piece of literature. That's why faith-sharing skills are essential, especially for your team members who will lead breaking open the Word sessions and other gatherings. Faith sharing will help the catechumens and candidates—and all of us—connect Scripture to their daily lives.

The steps below will help you go beyond exegesis, theology, or doctrine by calling you to connect your group's insights and study of Scripture to their own personal situation. Lastly, it helps you get to the "so what" conversion question: What difference does this Scripture passage make in our life today?

Practice the process below with your RCIA team members. You can do it as part of a team gathering, in pairs, small groups, or all together if your team is not too large.

1. Begin by praying together. You can use the collect (opening prayer) for the Sunday readings you will be discussing.

2. Invite someone to read aloud the gospel for the Sunday. If participants have copies of the reading, ask them not to read along but just to listen with open ears, hearts, and minds. After the reading, spend a brief moment in silent reflection.

3. Invite another person to read aloud the gospel again. Participants can follow along if they have the text. Ask participants to circle or write down words and phrases from the reading that strike them.

4. In pairs, small groups, or all together, discuss the words or phrases that stood out in the gospel reading and why.

5. Do steps 2, 3, and 4 with the first reading for the Sunday.

6. If there is time and if desired, do the same with the psalm or the second reading.

7. Together, discuss what was happening in the biblical communities that the readings were originally trying to address. An assigned team member might share some prepared background information about the readings.

8. Discuss any other exegetical, theological, seasonal, or liturgical context for the readings.

9. In pairs, small groups, or all together, discuss what is happening in the life of your parish or in the world right now that needs to hear the message of these readings.

10. In pairs, small groups, or all together, discuss what is happening in your own life right now that needs to hear the message of these readings.

11. Based on your discussions and reflections, discern the message that God's word is trying to communicate to your community in this particular time and place.

12. Share some prayerful silence together to let the Spirit lead each person to a new insight for his or her life.

13. Journal or share with the group what concrete action or commitment you will take this week to live this Word in your life.

14. End with a prayer of thanksgiving for God's word.

RCIA 75.2: Training in the Area of Community

The word "community" often connotes positive feelings of harmony or being with people you like. That's certainly often the case. But true Christian community goes much deeper. The RCIA describes it as the place not only where catechumens and candidates are supported by sponsors, godparents, and the entire Christian community, but also where they

> learn to turn more readily to God in prayer, to bear witness to the faith, in all things to keep their hopes set on Christ, to following supernatural inspiration in their deeds, and to practice love of neighbor, even at the cost of self-renunciation. (75.2)

In the training discipline of community, a catechumen or candidate joins with the Christian community to learn how to live in hope and watch for the Spirit acting all around them. In the community they practice sacrifice for the sake of another and love of neighbor, even for those they might not agree with—even for their enemies.

The training required of this area can only be attained by spending significant time within the Christian community, meeting many different people in the parish and hearing their stories. Most importantly, living the Christian communal way of life is primarily learning how to forgive others and ask for forgiveness, especially of those we find difficult to love. This area of training challenges catechumens and candidates to show the Christian spirit in their attitudes and actions in their own homes, workplaces, and neighborhoods, especially when it may lead to rejection or persecution.

This is not an easy area of training for anyone, but it's absolutely necessary if we are to be known by our love.

Evaluating your parish hospitality

Good hospitality is the beginning of community. Here are some observation questions you can use to assess the quality of your community's hospitality. What other questions would you add?

- On Sundays, at weddings, funerals, baptisms, and parish meetings and events, are there people outside, at the doors, and inside greeting people as they arrive?

- Do people readily greet one another, especially newcomers, without being prompted?

- Would a visitor leave your parish gathering having been personally greeted, welcomed, and invited to return by at least one other person?

- Are restrooms, meeting rooms, front doors, and parking lot driveways clearly marked so that visitors know where to find them?

- Do you avoid code language in your bulletin or website, such as "RCIA" or "ICF dinner," that only an insider would understand?

- Can visitors easily find the parish phone number with area code or an email address and the name of someone to contact if they are new to the parish?

- Are the parking lot, gathering areas, restrooms, and church spaces clean and inviting?

- Do those in wheelchairs have easy access to all parts of the church grounds?

RCIA 75.3: Training in the Area of Worship

In this area of training, catechumens and candidates learn how to pray actively, consciously, and fully in the Sunday gatherings of the community, in the week-to-week opportunities for communal prayer with other Christians, and in their own daily lives.

As we said in chapter 1, the liturgies are the premier place for formation because it is where Christ is most fully present in the assembly, the minister, the Word, and the sacraments. This is especially true for catechumens and candidates because it is where the church,

> . . . like a mother, helps the catechumens on their journey by means of suitable liturgical rites, which purify the catechumens little by little and strengthen them with God's blessing. (RCIA 75.3)

The kind of training needed to learn this aspect of Christian life can only be accomplished by gathering with the community to pray on Sundays and during the week, by learning how to participate fully in prayer, even when one doesn't want to or the style of prayer or music might not be one's preference.

Catechumens also need to learn how to meditate on and share with others "their joy and spiritual experiences" (RCIA 67A). That is why RCIA 75.3 says that part of their ordinary training in this area is to be sent out or dismissed before the celebration of the Eucharist—so they can practice sharing their faith and joy, which they have received from Christ in the liturgy. Notice in RCIA 67A that what the catechumens do after they are dismissed from the Mass is not catechesis or a class, but faith sharing. (Baptized candidates are never dismissed with the catechumens from Mass. See sidebar, "Five things to know about dismissals," for more information.)

Five things to know about dismissals

1: Catechumens have a job to do. The reason catechumens are dismissed for the Mass after the homily is not because they cannot yet share in Communion. It is because they have a specific role in the worshiping assembly. As soon as people enter the order of catechumens, they have two important liturgical responsibilities. First, they participate in the Liturgy of the Word to hear the Word and be fed by Christ present in that Word and assembly. Second, they "share their joy and spiritual experiences" (RCIA 67A) that they received from Christ in that Word. Their dismissal after the homily is similar, then, to the dismissal the baptized receive at the end of Mass: "Go and announce the Gospel of the Lord." In a sense, the catechumens are being commissioned, sent out to do the second part of their job. Once they enter into the order of the faithful, their liturgical responsibilities will change as well (see #4 below).

2: Catechumens do this job for the entire period of the catechumenate. From the day they become catechumens until the day they are baptized, catechumens are dismissed after the homily whenever they are present at a Eucharist.

3: The time after the dismissal from Mass is not catechesis; it's a continuation of the liturgy. Dismissal is not a time for catechesis. It is a time for reflection, prayer, and faith sharing that flow from God's word. The leader is not a catechist. He or she only needs to be someone who loves the Word and the catechumens and can facilitate a prayerful reflection with them. This could be a youth minister, a First Communion catechist, a choir member, a lector, someone from the parish council, a Bible study participant, or a member of the Women's Guild. It could even be a catechumen who is almost ready to be baptized and has some experience with the dismissal gathering.

4: The baptized candidates are never dismissed with the catechumens. The baptized, by virtue of their baptism, have a different job to do than the catechumens because of their order. They are members of the order of the faithful. That means they have the right and duty to pray the prayers of the faithful. These prayers are the creed, the universal prayers (general intercessions), and the eucharistic prayer. Even though they cannot yet share in Communion, they exercise their priestly role by praying these prayers. Also, even if they are barely or poorly catechized, the baptized candidates are not dismissed to be catechized. The dismissal of catechumens is not for catechesis but for faith sharing. The baptized candidates, as with the catechumens, are learning their faith primarily by their participation in the Mass according to their order.

5. *Sometimes, dismissals aren't possible.* At times, for serious reasons, a catechumen cannot be dismissed because of a practical or pastoral reason. One example might be a catechumen who is a single mother with baptized children, and she does not want to leave her children alone. Or you have only one catechumen, which may make faith sharing challenging. Or you have no one from the community available to do faith sharing with the catechumen. In this last situation, you could still choose to dismiss the catechumen from Mass and ask the catechumen to reflect on his or her experience at home or wait to meet with someone after Mass is over to do some faith sharing. For the other situations, there is still value in recognizing the catechumen during the Mass. Use the brief exhortation at RCIA 67C. In that option, the catechumen is invited to stay, and the presider briefly states our prayerful hope for him or her.

RCIA 75.4: Training in the Area of Witness

The description of the last area of training is only one sentence in the RCIA, but it may be the most important part of discipleship that catechumens and candidates need to learn:

> Since the Church's life is apostolic, catechumens should also learn how to work actively with others to spread the Gospel and build up the Church by the witness of their lives and by professing their faith. (RCIA 75.4)

If the very reason the church exists is to evangelize, if baptism is for mission, then the catechumens and candidates absolutely must learn how to do this. You cannot wait to teach catechumens until after they are baptized. Even before they become members of the Body of Christ, even before they can profess the creed and the other prayers of the faithful, they are called to announce the Gospel by their words and actions. If they and the candidates don't learn how to do this, they will not have learned the very purpose of being baptized.

The Christian community should therefore take care to always invite catechumens and candidates to work with them for justice and peace in their neighborhood and for reconciliation and care for those who are most in need at the peripheries of our society. Training in this area needs to give catechumens and candidates opportunities to spend time with those who are on the fringes of society, those who are oppressed, and to get their hands dirty working with other people of goodwill to ease their suffering.

So that's the list. I can imagine the disappointed droop on some of your faces. I have that same look every time I see those workout videos neatly packaged right by my bedside. The training to be disciples, like the path Jesus gave to the young rich man, isn't easy or neat and tidy, and it's not going to be quick. But it will be rewarding even more than a beach-ready body would be. And the system for getting there actually won't be as hard as you think. It may even be easier than what you're trying to do now for your catechumens and candidates! That's what we'll look at in the next chapter.

Chapter 5

Your Parish Life Is the Syllabus

In the previous chapter, we saw how the curriculum for making mature disciples in the Christian way of life consists of training them in four key areas: word, community, worship, and witness (RCIA 75). In this chapter, we will see how catechumens and candidates "study" those four areas through a syllabus that is provided by the life and weekly work of your parish. This syllabus is a hands-on course, and in this apprenticeship, the catechumens and candidates learn how to be disciples by doing what disciples do alongside other disciples.

In the introduction, I called this turning RCIA "upside down," where we stop trying to get the community involved in the RCIA and instead we work on getting the RCIA involved in the community. First let's look at a typical "right-side-up" RCIA. This might sound familiar to some of you.

RCIA the Usual Way

Imagine that you're the RCIA coordinator and that your process consists of gatherings of your catechumens, candidates, sponsors, and RCIA team members every Wednesday night in the parish hall. These gatherings include prayer, fellowship, and catechesis on some specific topic. Catechumens, candidates, and sponsors are required to attend; otherwise they'd have to make up a session with you or a team member at some other point.

You notice you don't have enough sponsors, and the parishioners you ask say they can't make that weekly commitment. So you make several pleas at Mass calling for volunteers, but you still end up sponsoring a few people yourself, as do several members of your RCIA team.

Every Sunday at the 10:30 a.m. Mass, the catechumens are dismissed and they spend about a half hour with one of your team members in faith sharing and breaking open the Word. You have a great team, but it's small, and the members you do have are feeling a little overwhelmed. So you make another announcement at Mass asking for people to join the RCIA team. One person responds, but doesn't feel comfortable leading faith sharing.

On the bright side, you've got all your Wednesday night presenters lined up for the next four weeks, but after that, there are a bunch of gaps. And although the seminarian is a really good guy, his skills and experience are still a bit limited. The pastor loves presenting for the RCIA, but his schedule is packed. Maybe you could get someone from the women's prayer group to come to one of your Wednesday night gatherings and talk about the rosary. You contact someone in that group, but Wednesday nights are when they meet, so that's a no-go.

One of the rites is coming up, so you put up pictures of the catechumens and candidates in the church vestibule and put an announcement in the bulletin asking people to pray for them, especially for those celebrating the next rite. Still, you hear the complaints and questions from parishioners at Mass wondering who all these people are and why they keep making their Mass long. You keep your hopes up. Maybe if you made prayer cards with a picture of each of the catechumens and candidates, and handed them out to the parishioners, that would help. It does, a bit.

To manage this model of RCIA, you have to reserve the hall every Wednesday, schedule the topics, get your presenters, lead the prayer, find someone to bring refreshments, set up the room, and clean up after. And you have to do all this every week because you've committed to a year-round RCIA.

For Sundays, you need to make sure you have someone from your team ready to lead faith sharing and breaking open the Word. We haven't even talked about the discernment meetings and discussions, training sponsors, planning retreats, and returning those voice messages from people asking to become Catholic in the middle of the year.

Whew! I'm exhausted for you! Now let's see what RCIA looks like when we turn it upside down.

RCIA Upside Down

In your upside-down RCIA, you meet all together with the catechumens, candidates, sponsors, and team members once a month for fellowship, prayer, and mystagogical catechesis. You and your team can handle preparing all the logistics for that monthly meeting because your large-group sessions take place only twelve times a year.

During the other weeks of the month, your sponsors are taking their catechumen or candidate to some parish activity, meeting, or diocesan event, each week if possible. This is scheduled between the sponsor and the catechumen or candidate according to their own calendars and interest. You also give the sponsors some ideas on events taking place that month in the parish or diocese and which activities might help their companion most in their training. If they're unable to join in on something happening at the parish or diocese any given week, they just get together for coffee or a meal. Or they check out the latest discussion, blog post, or inspirational video on the parish's Facebook page or webpage, and they share some thoughts about it with each other. Of course, every Sunday you'll find your catechumens, candidates, and sponsors at Mass with the community.

You ask the sponsors to send you an email or voice message every couple of weeks or so letting you know how things are going with their companion. By the way, each person has more than one sponsor because your catechumens and candidates have gotten to know so many people in the parish by going to all these events throughout the year that you have an abundance of people wanting to accompany them on their faith journey.

About once a week, you notice you also get some phone call or email message from someone in the parish who lets you know how delighted he or she was to spend time with one of the catechumens at last week's Bible study or the parish picnic or whatever event it was they were at. In fact, just last week you received a lovely handwritten thank-you card from the chair of the women's prayer group. A few of your catechumens and candidates decided to join their Wednesday night meeting a few weeks ago, and the ladies were so moved by their witness to their faith. In her message, the chair shares with you some of the comments from the women of how they saw God acting in the lives of those catechumens and candidates. Nice! That card goes into a folder with all the other notes you've received from other team members, parish staff, sponsors, and parishioners about your catechumens and candidates.

You notice an email from the lector coordinator. It's the list of lectors who will be helping to facilitate the Sunday faith sharing and breaking open the Word sessions for the coming month. He also adds a comment about how nice it was for Erica, one of your catechumens, and her sponsor to be part of the lector's monthly prayer and practice meeting. Their presence and comments added so much to the lectors' discussion, and the lectors themselves were inspired by Erica's story of answering God's call to baptism. It fit right in with one of the readings the lectors were reflecting on that night, and the coordinator noticed that the lectors practiced that reading a bit more just to get it right. He asks you to let Erica and her sponsor know that the lectors are praying for them.

Anna, one of your candidates who is being received into the Catholic Church this weekend, and her sponsor had volunteered a few weeks ago at the diocesan nursing home, which is down the street from your parish. There they met many of the families of those living at the nursing home. Several of them are parishioners. One of them stopped you after Mass last Sunday and said how much her family is looking forward to celebrating next week's rite for Anna. They all had met her at the nursing home and just loved how joyful she was with their mother, who lives there.

At the monthly RCIA gathering, your lead catechist facilitates a mystagogical reflection of how the catechumens and candidates encountered God this past month. They and their sponsors eagerly share with the group all the various parish activities they went to, what they saw and heard, what it taught them about being Catholic, and some of the questions that came up for them from their experiences. The discussion just keeps going and going! You pay close attention to the questions and insights they share and write them down in a journal. You'll use one of those questions or insights to create the outline for the next month's catechetical gathering. After the mystagogical reflection, you lead a brief presentation on the church's teaching on the saints because one of the questions that came up last month was on what makes a person a saint. The evening ends with the parish choir, who've been rehearsing for Sunday in the room next door, coming in to the hall after their rehearsal to lead everyone in singing the Litany of the Saints.

You get the idea. Upside-down RCIA is way more effective—and a lot more fun! Not only are the parishioners truly involved in the RCIA, but they are the ones leading the catechumens and candidates (and one another) to deeper conversion and renewal. Most of all, you'll avoid burnout for yourself and your team.

The Parish Bulletin: Your Weekly Resource for RCIA Formation

If you're going to work on getting your RCIA involved in the life of the community, you'll need to know what your parish and diocese are doing week after week. How do you find that out? You go to the bulletin, of course!

Let's check out a few activities from actual parishes across the United States. Listed here are a few things I found in their bulletins for the last week of June. That's a relatively slow time of year with many parish ministries or catechetical programs taking a break. Yet, there was still a ton of events going on in each parish that could be used as formation!

I've also matched these activities to the four areas of discipleship training found in RCIA 75. Some parishes are very strong in one or two of the four areas, but all of them have activities within each training discipline of RCIA 75. This helps you see how to personalize a training program for a catechumen or candidate in need of more experience in a particular area of discipleship. Of course, many of the activities could fit in more than one area. The point is to know what your parish is doing so you can tap into it.

Included in each of the bulletins were your typical activities that you would expect in a Catholic church, such as daily Masses, opportunities for confession, and prayer requests for the sick. I did not include these standard activities in the charts below, but be sure to use them and not to overlook these readily available opportunities! Instead, I highlighted activities or events that seemed particularly interesting or unique that would be powerful opportunities for formation.

I hope it's clear by now, too, that Sunday Mass should be the one parish event everyone participates in every week. Without it, no formation happens. Don't worry if your catechumens and candidates can't go to any other event in your parish that week. Just be sure they go to Sunday Mass.

Finally I give a brief description of each parish so you can see how each community, whatever its size, location, or demographic, has the gifts and resources it needs to provide a comprehensive and complete syllabus for training Christian disciples.

Saint Elizabeth Ann Seton: Houston, Texas

Saint Elizabeth Ann Seton is a multicultural mega-parish with an elementary school and is located in a suburb of Houston. The parish celebrates ten weekend Masses (six in English, three in Spanish, one in Vietnamese). The parish is known for its strong prayer and devotional life and offers many opportunities for ongoing adult spiritual formation.

Word (RCIA 75.1)	Community (RCIA 75.2)	Worship (RCIA 75.3)	Witness (RCIA 75.4)
Bible study in Spanish Parish mission gatherings Catechetical audio recording of the week Catechetical discussion on the relics of St. Maria Goretti (on her feast day); the parish altar contains her relics	Prayer intentions for those in the military Knights of Columbus tamale sale Annual parish garage sale Women's ACTS Retreat Men's group for those living with addiction	Charismatic prayer group Summer choir for Mass Divine Mercy Chaplet in Spanish Family Holy Hour in Spanish Night Offices of the Sacred Heart	Candlelight procession with the image of Our Lady of Fatima Archdiocesan youth conference Helping Hands Ministry assisting families with preplanning funerals Parish eldercare ministry

Saint Thomas Aquinas: Monterey Park, California

Saint Thomas Aquinas is an urban parish in the Los Angeles Archdiocese with about 1,200 families and a parish elementary school. There are five weekend Masses (three in English, one in Spanish, one in Chinese). The parish is proud of its cultural diversity and is known for its many community celebrations and sharing of Catholic cultural traditions.

Word (RCIA 75.1)	Community (RCIA 75.2)	Worship (RCIA 75.3)	Witness (RCIA 75.4)
Chinese and English Bible study Catechist training for First Communion	Community ping-pong Folk dance gathering Quinceañera setup and celebration Ignite youth group Parish dinner and dance	Chinese choir rehearsal Hispanic liturgy committee meeting Church renovation community meeting	Youth Legion of Mary Mandarin Legion of Mary

Blessed Trinity Catholic Community: Missoula, Montana

In 2006, Blessed Trinity was established near downtown Missoula as a blended parish of two communities and a rural mission. It's a smaller but thriving parish with three English Masses on the weekend (two at the parish and one at the mission). It is known in the diocese for its vibrant and excellent liturgies.

Word (RCIA 75.1)	Community (RCIA 75.2)	Worship (RCIA 75.3)	Witness (RCIA 75.4)
Parenting lecture series at neighboring parish Whole parish faith formation Diocesan women's retreat	Parishioner ninetieth birthday celebration Lunch Bunch social group Youth group summer movie series	Byzantine Divine Liturgy Sts. Peter and Paul feast day Mass Daily prayer book resources	Prayer shawl ministry Family Promise interfaith ministry assisting homeless families Missoula food bank volunteers

Saint Monica: Santa Monica, California

Being near the beaches of Los Angeles, the parishioners of Saint Monica tend to be more affluent, although the neighborhood has many people who are homeless and living in poverty. The community's commitment to serving those in need has attracted eight thousand families. With an elementary and high school, the parish celebrates six English Masses each weekend.

Word (RCIA 75.1)	Community (RCIA 75.2)	Worship (RCIA 75.3)	Witness (RCIA 75.4)
Marriage info night for anyone thinking of getting married	Coffee bar and gift shop	Rosary and Mass for peace in honor of Mary, Queen of Peace	Legion of Mary
Vacation Bible school	Parish volunteer appreciation dinner and awards	Centering prayer	Gay and lesbian outreach
Theology on Tap	Older adults beach hike and lunch	Monthly contemplative prayer night	Mission trip to sister parish in Kenya
GoodNews People retreat and weekly faith sharing	Summer Fellowship Fridays of Fun	Mass audio/ visual ministry	Justice ministries information night
Parishioner reflections in the bulletin		Lector gathering	JustFaith
			Meals at transitional
			Loaves and Fishes food drive

Got a year-round parish?
Then you have a year-round RCIA!

Lots of RCIA teams have fretted about trying to move to a year-round process. If your model of RCIA is the usual way described at the beginning of this chapter, then I'd fret too! Remember, the principal place of formation is the gathering of the assembly in liturgy. If your parish has Mass on Sunday, or some other kind of liturgical gathering if no priest is available, then you've got year-round RCIA! As long as your catechumens and candidates are coming to Mass every Sunday that your parish gathers, you have a year-round formation process. If there are other things going on in your parish during the week, even better!

The most important thing to remember when planning to do year-round RCIA is that discipleship training doesn't happen in a classroom. It's happening wherever your parishioners gather to be Christians together. And it happens primarily at Sunday Mass.

As inquirers show up throughout the year, don't stress about getting them caught up with sessions. Just put them where your parishioners are doing activities of word, community, worship, and witness, and let their work together begin your seekers' formation.

Size Doesn't Matter: Small Parishes

"Your ideas sound great for big city parishes, but I come from a small rural parish. Our parish doesn't have any activities."

Sometimes an RCIA team member will say something like that when I tell him or her that the parish activities are the syllabus for RCIA formation. Maybe you're thinking the same about your parish because none of the activities I've listed so far happen in your small community.

It cannot be true that any parish, no matter how small, has no activities. If you have enough people willing to give time, talent, and treasure to keep the lights on and the doors open, something must be going on.

At the very least, even tiny parishes have Sunday liturgy, funerals, Communion for the sick, anointing of the sick, possibly weddings, probably parish dinners or socials, maybe a communal rosary, adoration, parish council meetings, maybe a choir, finance council meetings, Stations of the Cross, church cleaning and decorating committees, Communion ministry, lector ministry, preaching, probably infant baptism, probably First Communion, reconciliation services during Lent, access to diocesan workshops and retreats, maybe a quilting or knitting circle, maybe a men's group like Knights of Columbus, a priest with a story to tell, a longtime married couple with a story to tell, new parents or grandparents with a story to tell, access to services from Catholic Charities, fasting, maybe a Thanksgiving food drive or Christmas clothing drive . . .

If your parish exists, something is going on there.

Here are a couple of small parishes where formation is happening just because they exist as parishes.

Saint Anthony of Padua: Atlanta, Georgia

Saint Anthony of Padua is a small urban parish of 380 families, located in the West End of Atlanta. The neighborhood has been in economic decline for many years but is recently experiencing a revitalization in business and the arts. There are two weekend Masses serving the predominantly African-American community, known for its incredible hospitality and spirit-filled worship. Here are some events happening in their small but vibrant community.

Word (RCIA 75.1)	Community (RCIA 75.2)	Worship (RCIA 75.3)	Witness (RCIA 75.4)
ALPHA follow-up lunch

Archdiocesan retreat | Men's health and well-being group

Finance council meeting | Adoration

Parishioner-written parish prayer for the week in the bulletin | Praying for families with prenatal diagnosis

Black Lives Matter meeting

Free community lunch to anyone in need

Free haircuts for children going back to school |

Still not small enough for you? Try this.

Saint Rose of Lima: Wrangell, Alaska

This is the oldest parish in Alaska, located in southeast Alaska in the Diocese of Juneau. The parish website doesn't say how many parishioners are registered, but based on photos, you might be able to fit fifty people into the church. Another parish in the diocese boasts twenty registered families, so I'd guess St. Rose might be about the same. They have two Masses on Sunday and a weekday Mass on Monday and Tuesday most weeks of the year. Here's what you'll find on their website and one-page bulletin.

Word (RCIA 75.1)	Community (RCIA 75.2)	Worship (RCIA 75.3)	Witness (RCIA 75.4)
Men's Bible study and breakfast on Thursdays at the Presbyterian church Women's Bible study	Fellowship luncheon every Sunday after the 11:00 a.m. Mass Christmas children's pageant	Installation of the new diocesan bishop	Help with lawn maintenance

What's in Your Bulletin?

Next time you're at your church or on its webpage, check out your parish bulletin, and start noticing all the RCIA formation opportunities ready and waiting for your catechumens and candidates. Use a chart like the ones above and begin listing all the different activities under the four discipleship areas of word, community, worship, and witness. As you do this, you might begin to notice not only new ways to train your seekers but also areas of strength—and weakness—in your own parish life. Which discipleship areas are already strong in your parish, and which ones could use some attention?

In the next chapter, we'll look at the most effective way to teach this syllabus and to connect the experience of your catechumens and candidates to the teaching of the church.

Chapter 6

When Do We Get to the *Real* Teaching?

I *love* taking classes and learning from professors. I especially love theology and exploring how Christians understand God. If I could, I'd be a student for life, spending my days reading and going from one professor to the next, soaking in as much of their wisdom as I can.

For some of us, that kind of teaching and learning about our faith is exactly what gets us out of bed each day. For a whole lot of people who got into RCIA and catechetical ministry, that desire for understanding faith is why we do what we do. We want so much to instill that thirst for knowledge of God and faith in those we teach.

Here's the deal, though. This kind of teaching works only if the people who are learning *already love* God and *love* the people of God. Receiving knowledge from a book or a teacher builds upon the love and faith that is already there in the learner and deepens that love and faith in the heart of the disciple.

Remember Rocio from the introduction? If I had immediately put her into a classroom when she first came to us and gave her a book to read, she may have *learned* some information, but she wouldn't have *known* God. Thankfully, her encounters with the

Christian community, especially in their apostolic witness to those orphans in Tijuana, broke open her heart so that the Holy Spirit could plant the seed of faith there. As her connection with the Christian community grew through her daily interactions with them, so did that love and faith in Christ. Only then could the information I was trying to give her draw her deeper into that "way of faith and conversion" (RCIA 1) that is the life of discipleship.

As theologians who help others know God and our Christian faith, we need to remember that our goal—for our seekers and ourselves—must always be deeper love for God in Christ.

Why Your RCIA Process Needs a Theologian . . . and Why That's You

You might not think you're a theologian. But if you've ever tried to answer the questions, "Who is God?" or "Why does God matter?" then you've done theology.

These big "meaning of life" kinds of questions often lie beneath the questions seekers, catechumens, and candidates ask. Our job as RCIA teams is to answer those questions in a way that makes sense for them in language and at a level they can understand. But don't reach for your copy of the *Summa* or the Catechism just yet!

What Is Theology?

Theology is different from other academic disciplines such as philosophy, biblical studies, or religious studies even though theology overlaps with them in many ways.

- Theology incorporates many philosophical questions and methods.

- Theology looks to the Bible for insights into God's identity.

- Theology includes an awareness of the historical and sociological development of what people believe about God and how they live.

Yet the biggest difference with theology is that the theologian is striving to know God intimately, not just study God from a distance.

The earliest disciples had an intimate, direct knowledge of God in Jesus Christ. Their personal encounters with Jesus and what they observed when he walked and ate with them became their lens for understanding who God was and how they were to live in the world. Their personal relationship with Christ gave meaning to their lives when they were being persecuted and martyred for their faith. And their response of faith to the questions of their day gave them further insights into the mystery of God.

Knowing About versus Believing In

However for people like us, living thousands of years after Christ's ascension, how do we know God whom we have never observed with our own eyes?

Here is where the gift of faith comes in. In faith, we can know God not as an intellectual pursuit but in the same way we know love, loss, joy, or disappointment. Faith is what differentiates theology from academics. The theologian is first a person who believes in God and has a relationship with God. That faith and love compel the theologian to want to know more about God, especially who God is for us in this particular time and place.

Saint Anselm described theology as "faith seeking understanding," and what we are trying to understand is not a doctrine but a person—God. The demons who recognized Jesus understood the doctrine of the Son of God (Matt 8:28-34), but the man born blind believed in him (John 9:1-41).

Interpreting the Signs of the Times

Faith allows the theologian to serve as a translator who stands on the boundary between our profound experience of the mystery of God and the real-life human situation in which we live. The theologian stands in the middle to "co-relate" the border between the divine and all of humanity's deepest questions.

When the theologian focuses too much on the divine, he or she risks making theology a discipline of doctrinal fundamentalism or historical archaeology.

On the other hand, if he or she concentrates only on the human question and longing, then theology becomes counseling or political science or simply one's own spirituality.

Between Here and There

RCIA teams stand in this middle. We bear the great responsibility of translating, interpreting, and helping seekers like Rocio see the world in which they live through the eyes of faith. We also have the great gift of presenting the longings and needs of our seekers to God whom we believe by faith will heal them and draw them closer to him in love. When we do this, we make the mystery of God no less mysterious but all the more knowable.

Mystagogy: Savoring the Mystery of God

God is a mystery, but not like an Agatha Christie novel or a math problem to be solved.

God is a mystery in the way that your grandmother's love is a mystery; in the way your child is the most beautiful creature God ever made; in the way you marvel at how much more in love you are with your spouse even after so many years.

God is also a mystery in the way that death, loss, and suffering are mysteries. The moments that take us into the depths of human joy and grief are where we first realize there is something bigger and deeper than what we can imagine.

In these moments, we can feel immensely close to God and at the same time so insignificant in the presence of God's grandeur. There is no way to fully express this feeling or describe it to another person. We can only say what we tell our children who ask, "How will you know when it's love?": You'll know it when it happens to you. But there is a way to reflect on this mystery and let it shape our lives.

Reflecting on the Mysteries

The word "sacrament" comes from the same Greek root for the word "mystery." Often, at the beginning of Mass, the priest will say, "to prepare ourselves to celebrate these sacred mysteries . . ." Every time we gather to celebrate the sacraments, we enter deeply into the mysterious love of God.

We experience this divine mystery most fully in the Eucharist—that intimate act of eating and drinking together the Body and Blood of the one we love the most: Christ.

Those who have been initiated into Christ—baptized, confirmed, and welcomed to the eucharistic table—are named "Christ." They are those who have most fully been immersed into God's mysterious love. Now, they know what it means to be a member of the Body of Christ because they have experienced it for themselves.

Anyone who is new to love needs time to reflect on what happened to them. This "looking backward" to a specific moment when they experienced God's mysterious presence gives them direction and renewed commitment for moving forward. Just like looking back at wedding pictures can give us more hope and joy for the future, reflecting on the experience of the "mysteries"—the sacraments—can renew our commitment to live according to Christ's name, which was given to us at baptism.

Yet this remembering is not like recalling the things of the event. It's more about remembering the person we encountered in the event. Christ's presence through the Holy Spirit is the only reason the event can and does change us. Our reflection on the event helps us grow deeper in love with Christ.

A Step-by-Step Guide to Mystagogy

This process is called *mystagogy*. Many of us think of mystagogy as the final period of the catechumenal process, occurring in the fifty days after the Easter Triduum. But mystagogy is for all our days. From the very beginning, our encounters with the inquirers and later the catechumens and candidates should be mystagogical.

That mystagogical reflection continues, whether we were baptized last year or many years ago. All of us are called to constantly reflect on our experience of God, discern its meaning, renew our commitment to our baptismal promises, and commit ourselves to living those promises in the ordinary events of our daily life.

It might help to break apart the word a little. The root of "mystagogy" is "agogy," which comes from the Greek word *agogos*. That means "leader." So pedagogy, for example, is about leading (or teaching) children. A synagogue is a gathering place (syn: "together") to which people are led. Mystagogy is a process of leading (or training) into the mystery. Mystagogy is initiation into that which is not yet fully revealed.

Even more specifically, mystagogy is an initiation into God's self-revelation. We've all experienced God's revelation. If you think about it, you can probably recall something that happened to you just a moment ago that you'd identify as God acting in your life. Certainly you've experienced an act of God within the last twenty-four hours. God is acting all the time. God is in every breath we take and every blink of our eyes. It's not as though God chooses some obscure moment to break into our lives with thunderbolts or floods. Just the opposite. God is so present that we sometimes take the ongoing, constant revelation of God for granted. We have to actively remember how God has been acting in our lives to fully see.

So try this.

At your next team meeting, start out by asking everyone, "How have you encountered God this week?" That question is mystagogical. It leads us deeper into the mystery, or ongoing revelation, of God.

Mystagogy with inquirers and catechumens. If we are doing mystagogy with inquirers, instead of other Christians, the inquirers set the agenda. We ask them, in various ways, how they have encountered God in their lives. We help them explore their experiences of God, and, with the guidance of the Holy Spirit, gradually lead them to connect those experiences with the stories and traditions of the church. But this process is spontaneous and unstructured, led by the promptings of the Spirit.

When the inquirers become catechumens and move into the catechumenate, the process changes. Now, instead of spontaneous promptings of the Spirit that lead to revelation, we provide systematic and regular experiences of revelation. The schedule for this systematic revelation is the celebration of the liturgical year in the Sunday assembly. The liturgical proclamation of God's word over the course of the year "unfolds the entire mystery of Christ" (*Universal Norms on the Liturgical Year and the General Roman Calendar*, 1).

When the inquirers move into the catechumenate, the question, "How have you encountered God?" shifts as well. We ask more specifically, "How have you encountered Christ in the liturgy this week?" We can ask that question in a variety of ways, but the goal is to lead them into the mystery in a less spontaneous, more systematic way by beginning with the liturgy. We also can ask the same questions of their encounter with Christ in the life of the parish this week.

This mystagogical process can also be done with baptized candidates, especially from their encounter with Christ in the Sunday Mass. Although they do not yet share in Communion, they are still being shaped by the prayers of the assembly of the faithful and by their own participation in these prayers, especially their sacrifice of praise in the eucharistic prayer. It also happens wherever two or three Christians gather together to do what Christians do over the course of that year, for there in their midst is Christ. Therefore, the entire life of your parish, regulated by the liturgical seasons, are experiences of God's revelation and thus opportunities for mystagogical reflection.

Getting to the meat of it all. What happens next is very important. When we ask catechumens how they have encountered God, their responses will be true but incomplete. They are still learning to experience the mystery of Christ more fully. We ourselves still have scales on our eyes and plugs in our ears, but we have been given the gift of sight and the gift of hearing through the grace of baptism.

Even more importantly, we have been schooled in the tradition of the church. So we rely not only on our own ability to discern

God's presence but also on the teachings of the apostles and saints who have gone before us. Our job as catechists is to bring all this remembering to bear in the exploration of God's revelation this week in the liturgy and parish life.

So the mystagogical catechesis for catechumens and candidates looks like this:

1. *Encounter:* Participate fully, consciously, and actively in the Sunday liturgy and in the life of the parish to encounter Christ in a profound way.

2. *Recollect:* Recall how you encountered Christ in that event. What happened? What did you see, hear, and do? Listen to what others remember, especially your sponsor, catechist, and those who have been given insight into the mystery through baptism.

3. *Reflect:* What was the most memorable moment of that encounter with Christ? How did that make you feel? Feelings, both positive and negative, are promptings of the Spirit because we can't control them. They are the Spirit's way of getting our attention. What do you think the Holy Spirit was trying to show you and say to you in that moment?

4. *Catechesis:* With the catechist and others who have been schooled in the church's tradition, explore what the apostles and saints have taught us about this particular encounter with Christ. What are some texts from Scripture and other sacred writings that relate to that encounter? What Christian traditions, prayers, and disciplines do we practice to strengthen and deepen our understanding of that teaching?

This fourth step is where the catechist stands at the boundary between our profound experience of the mystery of God and the real-life human situation. It's where we do theology and "co-relate" the catechumen and candidate's encounter with Christ to the story of our Christian tradition. This is the "meat" of catechesis that helps the catechumens and candidates break open their spiritual experiences of Christ in the assembly of the faithful.

However, only if we begin with the catechumen and candidate's encounter with Christ will this catechesis lead them to that "profound sense of the mystery of salvation in which they desire to participate" (RCIA 75.1).

There are two more steps if we want to help the catechumens and candidates integrate this new understanding into their practice of faith and discipleship:

5. *Connect:* Having remembered how we have encountered Christ in the liturgy, our parish life, and the teaching of the apostles and saints, what is happening in our world right now that needs to remember this experience? How is God calling our community to be more credible in our witness? What is the Spirit calling me to change in my life so I can be a more faithful disciple?

6. *Convert:* What will I commit to doing this week to live as a disciple of Christ in the world? What change can I make to be more like Christ for others?

This mystagogical reflection of the catechumens and candidates in the midst of the Christian community draws them deeper into the love of God as they prepare to encounter Christ again and again in the liturgy and the life of disciples.

Mystagogical Catechesis

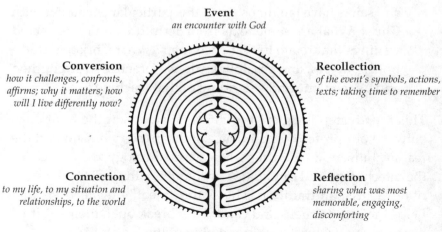

Event
an encounter with God

Conversion
how it challenges, confronts, affirms; why it matters; how will I live differently now?

Recollection
of the event's symbols, actions, texts; taking time to remember

Connection
to my life, to my situation and relationships, to the world

Reflection
sharing what was most memorable, engaging, discomforting

Catechesis
what Scripture and Tradition teach us;
what we can learn from the symbol, action, text

If we do this kind of teaching regularly, week after week, if we begin with a profound encounter with Christ, honor the experience of the catechumen and candidate, connect their experience to the teaching of the church, and call them to deeper conversion, then we can expect the catechumens and candidates to acquire an appropriate understanding of our faith that will increase their love for God in Christ and their unity with the church.

Ongoing Catechesis

This mystagogical process is intended for all Catholics as a lifelong catechesis because we still see only dimly, as St. Paul says. It is through the ongoing liturgical celebration of the mystery and the lifelong systematic exploration of our encounter with the mystery that the scales are lifted from our eyes.

That lifelong catechesis begins at baptism and confirmation where the catechumens are given the insight of the royal priesthood of Christ. With that grace, they are brought to the table to eat and drink the full presence of Christ in a way they have not yet fully encountered. The fifty days of Easter are a time for these neophytes and for all the baptized to focus specifically on remembering that initiation into the banquet of the Lamb in a systematic way. Even more intensely than in their catechumenate, mystagogy for neophytes is first and foremost a liturgical experience that takes place in the midst of the Sunday assembly. It is there, with their eyes and ears newly opened by the sacraments, that they see and hear Christ in a new way—as priestly people united to his sacrifice.

Flowing from that encounter with the mystery of Christ in the liturgy, the neophytes might gather once or twice during the Easter season specifically to remember and explore the experience of their initiation in the sacraments. The systematic, initiatory catechesis focused on training them in those four areas of discipleship in RCIA 75 had ended with their entrance into the period of purification and enlightenment at Lent. Now, beginning with Easter Sunday and continuing for the rest of their lives, the neophytes enter into the ongoing adult faith formation process of the rest of the baptized. And that process is, of course, mystagogical.

Sponsors as mystagogues

Catechists are best able to lead catechumens or candidates through the mystagogical process and substantially nourish them with the church's teaching flowing from the catechumens' or candidates' experiences. But you don't need a master's degree to have a mystagogical conversation. Anyone with faith in God and a relationship with Christ can ask mystagogical questions to stimulate a conversation that begins to break open an encounter with Christ.

Here are some questions that sponsors, team members, and parents can use any time to engage catechumens and candidates in a mystagogical conversation:

- What was your most memorable moment of that liturgy or event?

- What was your favorite part? (This question works well with children.)

- What did you see/hear/do/feel?

- What did it mean to you?

- What does it remind you of from the Bible or from our Catholic traditions?

- What does it tell you about God?

- What does it say about Christ?

- If that symbol could speak, what would it say to us about our faith?

- How does this change you?

Now that we've established a process for conversion-centered teaching, let's look at how to customize this catechesis for the many kinds of seekers we meet.

Chapter 7

Customized Catechesis

Three Levels of Catechesis

Many of the people we put into the RCIA are not like my friend Rocio at the Newman Center, who was a raw beginner, never having had any kind of experience of religion or God or the Christian community in her life when I met her.

In most of our RCIA processes, maybe we'll have a Rocio. We'll also have a mainline Protestant who knows more about Scripture than most Catholics and has been living as a disciple since childhood. Between these two, we'll have folks who are somewhat catechized. They may be unbaptized or baptized, they know who Jesus is, they pray, they know some of the more famous stories from Scripture, even if they have never read the Bible. But there are big gaps in both their knowledge of the faith and their practive of living as disciples. Then you'll get the anomaly who doesn't fit any of these descriptions! So how do we provide a suitable catechesis for a diverse group like this without burning ourselves or our team members out?

Two Paths; One Goal

Something that has really helped me sort things out is to think of two separate but related paths. When people come to us inquiring about the sacraments, we need to discern where they are on each path in order to provide the most suitable catechesis and to honor their ritual order in the church. These two paths are interdependent, and individuals always move forward in each of them at their own pace. Their place in one path doesn't always affect their place in the other. However, when there has been good and substantial discernment, the two paths might correspond at set points.

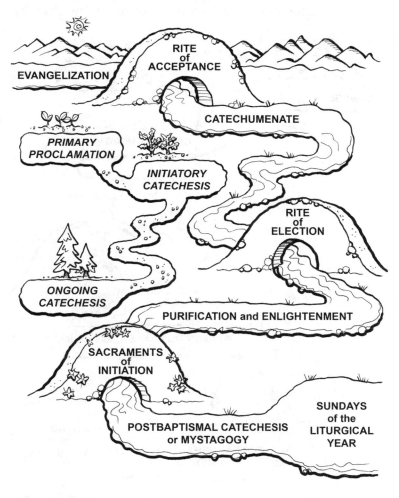

Using these two paths together, we see a clearer picture of the people before us and what they each need in order to become stronger Christian disciples, which is the goal for each path. Let's explore each of the two paths.

The Ritual Path

The ritual path for the unbaptized is made up of the stages and rites of part 1 in the RCIA (the ritual path for the baptized candidates may seem similar, yet their preparatory rites are optional and do not change their ritual status, or order, in the church):

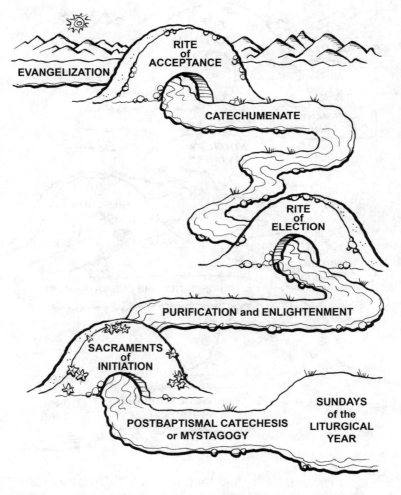

The **Period of Evangelization and Precatechumenate** prepares a person for the *Rite of Acceptance into the Order of Catechumens.* This rite changes the order of a person. They go from having no order or official status in the Church to being a member of the Order of Catechumens.

The **Period of the Catechumenate** and the rites belonging to this period prepare a person for the *Rite of Election*. This rite does not change a catechumen's order, but it does mark that person as one of the catechumens elected to be initiated at the next Easter Vigil.

The **Period of Purification and Enlightenment** and the rites belonging to this period prepare a person for the *Sacraments of Initiation* (baptism, confirmation, and Eucharist). Baptism changes a person's order from catechumen to being a member of the order of the faithful.

The **Period of Postbaptismal Catechesis or Mystagogy** deepens a person's faith to live as a lifelong disciple of Christ nourished by the Sunday celebrations of the Eucharist.

The three main rites (Acceptance, Election, Initiation) are like one-way doors. Once you go through them, you can't go back. So the periods in the ritual path prepare the person to enter the next doorway. (There is no "doorway" after the last period listed here, unless you want to imagine death as the final doorway completing our entrance into the eternal life begun at baptism.)

A person's location on the ritual path is determined by which rites they have celebrated:

- Unbaptized persons who have not yet celebrated the Rite of Acceptance, regardless of their knowledge of Christian faith or level of discipleship, are in the evangelization period.

- Validly baptized persons, regardless of their knowledge of Christian faith or level of discipleship, are in the postbaptismal period.

- Those who have entered the order of catechumens are somewhere in the middle two periods.

Ritually, there can be no baptized persons in the two middle periods because baptism by nature places one into the last period of this ritual path. Once baptized, we can never go backward on this ritual path and pretend we are catechumens again because this ritual path is about one's order—or ritual role—in the church.

The Catechetical Path

The catechetical path marks levels of catechesis. Like the ritual path, we cannot really go backward on it because we can't really "un-know" something once it's been proclaimed to us. We could certainly have forgotten it and would have to relearn it again, or we don't believe it and need more time to accept it. But those are essentially different than never having known it to begin with.

This path is also a bit more fluid than the ritual path. There are no rites on this path to demarcate where one is located on it, and there are varying degrees with each section of the path. We use the practice of discernment to determine where a person is along the catechetical path.

We can imagine the catechetical path like the gradual growth of a plant. The first level is at the seedling stage. In the second level, the seed has taken root and begins to thrive. At the third level, the plant has reached maturity and continues its ongoing growth.

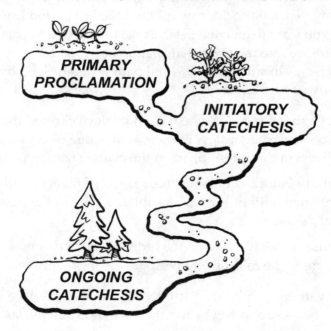

This catechetical path is outlined in the *General Directory for Catechesis,* chapter 2, where it describes each of the three levels of catechesis: 1) primary proclamation; 2) initiatory catechesis; 3) ongoing formation.

1. Primary proclamation (*General Directory*, 61–62): This level of catechesis is for those like Rocio, our complete beginner. It's not even really catechesis in the way we think of catechesis. It's more like proclamation. Rocio had never heard the message of Christ until somehow, some Christian did and said something that planted a seed of faith and moved her to knock on our Newman Center door. For people at this level, our goal is to proclaim the message of the Gospel in a way they can hear it and respond to it. That way is going to be at a radically human level that responds to the very basic human needs for love, belonging, hope, and healing.

To make this primary proclamation, we use the three levels of evangelization described by Pope Paul VI, which we reviewed in chapter 3:

- wordless witness by our actions and

- explicit witness through our words

- that leads to a connection with the Christian community as described in RCIA 9.1, where the baptized show the spirit of Christ to the inquirer in informal, spontaneous ways through conversation, home visits, and parish gatherings

Primary proclamation or evangelization is happening all the time, or at least that's what Christians are called to do. It's our baptismal mission that we live out every day in informal ways wherever we see people in need. Plus, it's always geared toward those who have never heard and believed the message that Jesus loves them.

Once a person like Rocio hears that message and begins to believe it, she inches closer on the *ritual* path toward that first doorway of the Rite of Acceptance. The things we do for her, as described at RCIA 9.1, are meant to strengthen her initial response to God's call and draw forth the marks of readiness for the Rite of Acceptance.

Look at the things your parish is doing that are responding to basic human longing and healing people's wounds. These would be things like the corporal and spiritual works of mercy.

It's these activities—not pre-theology classes, Catholic info nights, or mini-courses on the church—that will spark the beginnings of faith for those at this first level of catechesis.

We'll measure the level of the seekers' response to God and readiness for mission by using the discernment markers found at RCIA 42, which describe what we need to see in people before they can go through the first doorway, the Rite of Acceptance.

Discerning readiness for the Rite of Acceptance. These are the things we need to see and strengthen in seekers' lives before they are ready to celebrate the Rite of Acceptance (see RCIA 42):

- The beginnings of the spiritual life

- The basics of Christian teaching have taken root

- There is evidence of first faith

- We see the beginnings of a change in their lives

- They want to change their lives even more

- There is evidence of a sense of sorrow, dissatisfaction, or regret for how they have lived so far

- They start to pray

- They sense that being with other Christians is important

- They start to know some people in the parish through conversations, meals, and other gatherings

Who discerns their readiness for the Rite of Acceptance? (see RCIA 43):

- Sponsors (note that sponsors are joined to a seeker long before the Rite of Acceptance)

- Catechists

- Deacons

- Priests and pastors

Discernment is an act of prayer

It might seem daunting or even wrong to think that we could discern someone's readiness. Isn't that the Holy Spirit's job? Who are we to make such a decision?

When we feel this way, I think it's because we haven't clarified what we're doing in discernment. Sometimes, we equate discernment with deciding if God or the church accepts or loves these people. Of course God loves and accepts them, and so do the people of God.

Discernment, rather, is a prayerful listening to the Holy Spirit and a deep remembering of how we have seen God acting in their lives. What do we see and hear in them that tells us they are responding to God's action in their lives? The reason to listen and look carefully for God's action and their response to it is to determine if they are ready yet to do Christ's mission according to their place on the ritual path, that is, their order in the church.

If they're not yet ready, our job is to keep strengthening them with primary proclamation or with initiatory catechesis and most of all with love for them until they are equipped to respond to God and take on the mission of Christ.

You and the Christian community are exactly the right people to do this discernment because, through your baptism, you have been given the eyes and ears of faith to see and hear God acting in the world. So entrust your work of discernment wholeheartedly to the Holy Spirit, look for how God has been acting in their lives, discern ways to help them deepen their relationship with Christ, and give thanks for the Father's abiding love in their lives and in the community.

2. Initiatory catechesis (*General Directory*, 64–68): Once unbaptized seekers have manifested the marks of readiness to take on the responsibilities of being catechumens, and they are given a new role in the church through the Rite of Acceptance into the Order of Catechumens, the second level of catechesis begins. At this level, the initial seeds of faith begin to grow and develop through a complete and systematic catechesis.

The syllabus for this catechesis is RCIA 75. The methodology for teaching that syllabus is mystagogical catechesis. The ones who teach it are the entire parish community.

A person at this level of catechesis encounters the living Christ in four principal ways and learns the basic disciplines of the Christian way of life in these four areas of discipleship:

- Catechesis on the word that leads to an acquaintance with dogmas and precepts and to a profound sense of the mystery of salvation (RCIA 75.1)

- Communal life and the disciplines of sacrifice and self-renunciation (RCIA 75.2)

- Worship and prayer within the community (RCIA 75.3)

- Apostolic witness and profession of faith in word and deed (RCIA 75.4)

Baptized or unbaptized persons can be in this level depending on how much they need to learn or strengthen these four basic areas of discipleship.

This second level is not meant to be the total extent of a person's catechesis; it is simply *initiatory.* That is, it trains them to live as disciples and prepares them to take on the lifelong mission of Christ in the church and the world. So the extent of the catechesis at this level is very basic since initiation expects that one will continue with deeper, more advanced formation throughout one's life after baptism.

Review chapter 5 for ideas on how your parish community can form people at this level of catechesis. Choose *basic* activities in each of the four areas of RCIA 75. For example, in the area of word, a ten-week course on the book of Revelation is probably a bit too advanced for a person at the second level of catechesis. However, one of your faith-sharing groups that meets after Sunday Mass just might be perfect.

In addition, a person at this level may be very strong in a few of the areas of discipleship, but they're weak in the others. For example, Rocio was really strong in her practice of apostolic witness and community. But she didn't always make it to Sunday Mass, and she needed a lot more experience praying with and reflecting on Scripture. So for someone like her, you'd want to encourage her and her sponsor to participate in more of the parish's activities under word (RCIA 75.1) and worship (RCIA 75.3).

For catechumens or candidates at this level of initiatory catechesis, the purpose of the entire curriculum of formation is to help them be ready to profess their faith in God and to be a credible witness in the world to Christ.

Again, we'll measure their response to God's action in their lives and their readiness for mission. The discernment markers we'll use are found at RCIA 120 which describes what is necessary in the knowledge, attitudes, and behaviors of people before they can go through the second doorway, the Rite of Election.

Discerning readiness for the Rite of Election. These are the things we want to see and strengthen in catechumens' lives before they can be ready to celebrate the Rite of Election (see RCIA 120):

- They show "a conversion in mind and in action"; that is, they know what it means to be a disciple and they do it.

- They have "a sufficient acquaintance with Christian teaching," enough to support them in living out the four areas of discipleship.

- They exhibit "a spirit of faith and charity" through their hope, outlook on life, and love for others.

- They intend to be baptized, confirmed, and share in the Eucharist and to do so by their own will and desire.

- They are committed to stating their intention to live as lifelong disciples before the bishop and the church at the diocesan Rite of Election.

Who discerns their readiness for the Rite of Election? (see RCIA 121 and 122):

- Bishop
- Priests and pastors
- Deacons
- Catechists
- Godparents
- The entire community
- The catechumens themselves

Using sponsors more effectively

The RCIA doesn't say much about what sponsors do outside of their role at rituals. RCIA 9 says, "Sponsors are persons who have known and assisted the candidates and stand as witnesses to the candidates' moral character, faith, and intention."

Here are some specific ideas to help you use your sponsors more effectively in both catechizing catechumens and candidates and discerning their readiness:

1. Ask the sponsors to prayerfully reflect on the Sunday readings before coming to Mass. Ask them to teach their catechumen or candidate how to do the same. And ask the sponsors to follow up to make sure they are actually doing the preparation.

2. Make the sponsors responsible for the presence of their catechumen or candidate at Mass each week. If their companion has to be out of town, it should be the sponsor's responsibility to help him or her locate a parish to attend that weekend. Or if there is a scheduling conflict, the sponsor will be sure he or she gets to one of the other Masses in your parish or a neighboring parish.

3. Teach the sponsors how to ask their catechumen or candidate three mystagogical questions about the Sunday reading. The sponsors should also share their reflections on these questions with their catechumen or candidate:

- What did you see in the readings?
- What did you hear in the readings?
- What do these readings mean for your life?

4. If they will be able to "stand as witnesses to the candidates' moral character, faith, and intention," they will need to pay attention and listen to their catechumen or candidate. A daily practice of prayer and reflection will help attune their eyes to seeing God at work in their catechumen or candidate. They can use the three questions that the bishop will ask the godparents at the Rite of Election to help guide their prayerful reflections (RCIA 131B):

- "Have they faithfully listened to God's word proclaimed by the church?"
- "Have they responded to that word and begun to walk in God's presence?"
- "Have they shared the company of their Christian brothers and sisters and joined with them in prayer?"

Sponsors should regularly share their reflections with their catechumen or candidate and with the RCIA team on how they see God acting in the life of their companion.

3. Ongoing formation (*General Directory*, 69–71): All who are generally living out the faith through the four areas of Christian life belong in this third level of catechesis. Their faith has matured with strong roots in the Christian way of life. They have shown the basic skills of living a life of the Word and putting the Word into practice. They know how to sacrifice themselves for others and to encourage others with their hope and joy. They pray with the community on the Lord's Day and have a practice of prayer throughout the week. And they profess their Christian faith in the world through actions and words.

In their desire to deepen their love for God, they strive to grow in understanding of their Catholic faith. They do this through the following:

1. Scripture study

2. Christian reading of current events

3. Liturgical catechesis

4. Occasional catechesis

5. Spiritual formation

6. Systematic theological instruction (see *General Directory for Catechesis*, 71)

Notice that these are relatively advanced forms of learning. They are not basic-level skills as we found in the second level of catechesis.

All the baptized are called to engage in ongoing formation at this level *if they have mastered the basic skills of discipleship.*

Many, if not most, of the people in our parishes are at this third level of catechesis. This certainly includes parish leaders and practicing Christians who are active in their faith. It also includes Catholics who are regularly participating in Sunday Eucharist but, for whatever reason, may have missed being confirmed. It may even include unbaptized persons who have been living as disciples for many years but simply never got baptized!

For those who are properly in this third level of ongoing formation, the kind of catechesis we provide at the second or first levels would be insufficient because they're too basic. Those at the third level are already in love with God and with God's people, and they already know how to live as disciples. They want something more.

In many parishes, the RCIA is the only place where adult faith formation is happening. So we tell our community members, "If you want to learn more about your faith, come to the RCIA!"

If the majority of people in our RCIA processes are "advanced Christians," we tend to bypass the first and second levels of catechesis for those who need it and move everyone to the third level.

That's when we get the systematic theological instruction presented at an advanced level. We break out the video series, resource programs, and theological texts and these become our RCIA materials.

The outcome is that those like Rocio at the first level and those who are just beginning to learn the disciplines of faith at the second level of catechesis get lost in the mix. Then we wonder why they don't show up, or why they look bored or lost during the sessions. When they don't return after baptism, we either blame ourselves, thinking we didn't teach them enough, or we lament that "RCIA just doesn't work."

The challenge for all our parishes is to develop an effective adult faith formation process for those for whom the third level of catechesis is suitable and appropriate. Keep the RCIA focused on primary proclamation and initiatory catechesis for those at the first and second levels.

Using catechetical resources appropriately

I know. You've already spent a good portion of your RCIA budget on a whole set of videos or textbooks and lesson plans arranged by topic and neatly scheduled for the next year, and you're wondering if you can get your money back.

Resource programs, textbooks, and videos, even weekly breaking open the Word sessions and doctrinal lesson plans are great resources to have . . . but only if you use them at the appropriate level of catechesis for the person you're trying to teach.

Remember my beach-ready body videos from chapter 4, still in their original packaging sitting by my bed for the last year? Right now, I don't need a workout video. I need someone to give me a first-level-style proclamation to inspire me to get off my butt! I won't find that in these videos. In fact, I'd only feel depressed watching them because my body isn't ready to do the exercises in them.

Packaged programs alone that help you to communicate information about our Christian way of life through a lesson plan or video presentation or chapter sections, no matter how well done or thorough, can never provide that complete and systematic catechesis required by the RCIA for those who are just beginning to live the Christian way of life. These catechumens and some candidates are at a second level, or an "initiatory level," of catechesis. They may even be in that first level of catechesis, needing more evangelization.

Most advanced programs and resources are better suited for those who are at a third level of catechesis, or "ongoing catechesis." People at this level are seeking deeper understanding of what they already believe and practice.

So don't get rid of your programs. Instead, use them for ongoing formation for your catechists or for preparing those Christians becoming Catholic who are already living the Christian life and are already deeply in love with Christ. Use them for your Bible study or faith-sharing group, with parents who have children preparing for First Communion or confirmation, with adults who are baptized and catechized and are preparing for confirmation or marriage, for those on parish council or parish staff—basically, those who are already living their faith in the areas of word, community, worship, and witness and who want to deepen their faith and understanding about the Christian way of life. But don't use them for catechumens or candidates who are just beginning a life of discipleship.

Many Forms of God's Grace

Rocio, our unbaptized, uncatechized person at the first level of catechesis, is the ideal candidate for the process outlined in the first part of the RCIA. Her ritual and catechetical paths are clear, and we know exactly where to put her on each path—right at the beginning. But what about all the other kinds of people we meet on the way of faith and conversion? Let's meet some of them.

Alex: Baptized but Uncatechized

Alex was baptized in the Catholic Church when he was a baby. His family wasn't very committed to their faith, but his grandmother thought he should be baptized, just in case. Other than the day of his baptism, Alex never had any other connection to the church or any kind of religious community or practice. Now as an adult, Alex has been deeply touched by the work of Christians in his neighborhood with those who struggle in these hard economic times. He saw a huge sign at the Catholic church down the street that said, "Free food every Friday all day long. Come if you're hungry or just need a helping hand." He mentioned this to his uncle, who reminded him that Alex had been baptized Catholic. The next Friday Alex decided to check out the Catholic church and see if they would let him volunteer in some way. His experience with them over the last few months has led him to want to strengthen his baptismal faith and learn how to live as a Catholic.

- Alex's place on the ritual path: Period of postbaptismal catechesis or mystagogy

- Alex's place on the catechetical path: First-level primary proclamation

Some general notes about Alex's formation (these are not exhaustive): Once he shows the marks of readiness found at RCIA 42, you can begin to systematically train him in the four areas of discipleship, especially Sunday Mass. Do this for at least a full liturgical year. Use mystagogical catechesis, always referring to the meaning of his baptism. Alex might also celebrate some of the optional rites for the baptized found in the RCIA, such as the Rite of Welcoming. But we would honor his baptism and never equate him ritually with the catechumens. Alex is never dismissed with the catechumens but stays in the Mass. Celebrate confirmation and Eucharist once he has exhibited the marks of readiness found at RCIA 120. He could celebrate these at the Easter Vigil, although the US bishops do not recommend this (see the United States *National Statutes for the Catechumenate*, 26), or on any Sunday as soon as he is ready.

Fred: Baptized Practicing Lutheran

Fred was baptized as a child in the Lutheran Church and was confirmed as a teen. He was active in his Lutheran parish throughout his childhood and young adulthood. In college he majored in biblical studies and eventually received a PhD in Scripture. He now teaches at a Lutheran seminary. While in college, he had met and married Martha, a practicing Catholic. They raised their three children in the Catholic Church and participated in all their sacramental preparation programs. They pray daily at home. Fred attends a Catholic parish every Sunday with his family and is active in it. Fred's mom had never approved of his involvement with the Catholic Church. But she recently passed away, and now Fred wants to formalize his union with the Catholic Church and unify his family's faith.

- Fred's place on the ritual path: Period of postbaptismal catechesis or mystagogy

- Fred's place on the catechetical path: Third-level ongoing formation, with emphasis on areas of understanding and practice that are distinctly Catholic, as well as any of the four areas of discipleship that Fred might be weak in

Some general notes about Fred's formation (these are not exhaustive):
Fred's sponsor should be someone who is also at the third-level
of catechesis who may be able to answer more complex questions,
especially those regarding the distinctions between Lutheran and
Catholic tradition and teaching. Fred's time of formal preparation
is relatively short, and he can celebrate the Rite of Reception as
soon as he has had some time for instruction on any questions he
has about the Catholic Church and for discernment. We would
not make Fred wait until the Easter Vigil to be received, and he
would "not be asked to undergo a full program parallel to the
catechumenate" (see *National Statutes for the Catechumenate*, 32).
Instead, his reception would take place at a Sunday Eucharist as
soon as he is ready. Reception also includes confirmation.

George: Unbaptized but Practicing Disciple

George has been playing guitar for years in a Catholic parish
choir. He and his wife are members of the parish council, and
they cochair the annual parish fiesta. They have two daughters who are altar servers. George and his wife went to every
infant baptism and First Communion preparation process
for their daughters and now are doing confirmation preparation for their older child. George is a model Catholic except
for one detail no one knew. He had never been baptized! He
just never thought he needed to. And because he was playing
guitar at Mass every week, no one noticed that he never went
to Communion. Going to the confirmation sessions with his
daughter started to help him realize the beauty of the sacraments. Now he wants to make his discipleship official.

• George's place on the ritual path: Period of evangelization
and precatechumenate; George is ready to enter through the
first doorway (Rite of Acceptance) as soon as he and his sponsor have been prepared for the ritual

• George's place on the catechetical path: Third-level ongoing
catechesis

Some general notes about George's formation (these are not exhaustive): Although George is well catechized already in the four areas of discipleship, he still needs to celebrate all the rituals that move him from no official role to catechumen and from elect to neophyte. If George wanted to and permission was granted by the bishop, his time of formation after the Rite of Acceptance could be condensed and he could celebrate the required rites of election, scrutinies, and presentations outside of the normal time of Lent and Easter Triduum. George might not be as familiar with mystagogical reflection, so his sponsor and catechist would focus on doing this more regularly with him. As soon as he becomes a catechumen, George would normally be dismissed from Mass after the homily because of his ritual responsibility as a member of the order of catechumens.

Jen: Baptized Returning Catholic Needing Confirmation

Jen had been baptized Catholic as a baby, went to Catholic grade school and high school, and celebrated First Communion with her class in elementary school. She was active in her parish youth group throughout elementary school, but in high school her faith and practice began to wane, and she eventually stopped going to Mass for several years. Now in college, Jen misses her parish community and wants to regain her passion for her faith. She begins going to the local university parish and asks if she could be confirmed.

- Jen's place on the ritual path: Period of postbaptismal catechesis or mystagogy

- Jen's place on the catechetical path: Somewhere between second-level initiatory catechesis and third-level ongoing formation

Some general notes about Jen's formation (these are not exhaustive): Jen's ritual and catechetical paths aren't referenced in the RCIA. (The process for the baptized found in the RCIA is for adults who were baptized as infants "but did not receive further catechetical formation nor, consequently, the sacraments of confirmation and eucharist" [400].) Jen's preparation is found in a separate ritual text called the Rite of Confirmation. Her formation, however, will still include training in the four areas of discipleship and mystagogical catechesis that refers her back to her baptism and weekly sharing of the Eucharist. She may also need preparation for reconciliation. Jen is never dismissed with the catechumens. She also would never celebrate her confirmation at the Easter Vigil. Instead she celebrates it with the bishop or at her parish with her pastor (who needs to request delegation from the bishop) as soon as she is ready.

People like Jen might need lots of encouragement and brushing up and perhaps even a bit of first-level "new evangelization" kind of proclamation. But according to RCIA 400, they are not participants in the catechumenate since they have had some level of formation after baptism. Their hearts had already been opened to Christ at some point, and somewhere along the way they forgot and lost that intimate love for God and for God's people. On some level they are practicing the disciplines of Christian life but not very well or regularly. They will need ongoing formation, oftentimes remedial, but their catechetical and ritual status are not the focus of the RCIA.

In reality, the majority of people in our RCIA processes are people like Jen, and they really shouldn't be. Our ministry with them is more appropriately adult faith formation and reconciliation, not *initiation*.

Keep the RCIA Focused on the Unbaptized and Uncatechized

If we keep the RCIA focused primarily on the unbaptized, like Rocio, and on the baptized uncatechized, like Alex, we can more properly attend to their needs in both their ritual and catechetical paths. The next time you are challenged with trying to provide a suitable catechesis for a broad range of people in your RCIA process, consider focusing on your Rocios and Alexes and move those who need a higher or remedial level of catechesis into a separate adult faith formation process.

Conclusion

What If?

Pilgrims on the Journey

When the US bishops wrote *Our Hearts Were Burning Within Us*, they said that the parish *is* the curriculum. They believed that when parishes were vitally alive with adults fully and actively conscious of their baptismal mission, we would have Catholics who would "witness and share the Gospel in their homes, neighborhoods, places of work, and centers of culture" (17). I believe them because I've seen it happen.

On the Second Sunday of Advent in 2015, when Pope Francis asked every diocese in the world to open a door of mercy to inaugurate an extraordinary jubilee year of mercy, my husband and I were vacationing in Costa Rica. We were missing the opening of the holy door in our own Diocese of San Jose in California, so we decided to try to catch the opening of the holy door in the Archdiocese of San José, Costa Rica. The sign at the cathedral said the opening of the door would happen at 3:00 p.m., starting at a neighboring church about ten blocks away.

That afternoon, we walked to the church, expecting maybe a few hundred people. When we arrived, we saw people crammed at the doorways trying to get in. We heard music and singing inside. We squeezed our way through the crowd to the threshold of one of the side doors. There had to be at least two thousand people there including those standing in the aisles and outside each of the doors! A kind woman standing next to me noticed the bewildered look on my face and gave me her copy of the worship aid as she continued singing in Spanish along with all the people inside. I still couldn't believe it. All these people here, just to see a door opened on a Sunday afternoon!

After a brief homily by the archbishop, the deacon took the Book of the Gospels and followed two altar servers carrying incense and the cross down the center aisle to the main doors of the church. The crowd standing in the aisle parted like the Red Sea as pair after pair of altar servers carrying tall pillar candles on poles ten feet high, deacons, priests, bishops, and, finally, the archbishop made their way down the aisle and out the door. My bewilderment turned to awe as I saw the people—all two thousand of us—begin to follow after them.

Nick and I scrambled out the side door and hurried to the plaza in front of the church. The plaza was already filled with people. Somehow we made our way to the edge of the crowd toward the front of the procession. But soon, there would be no front, or back, or middle, just a sea of people moving shoulder to shoulder, step by step, down the boulevard through the capital city of downtown San José.

Out in the open, I could see our numbers had swelled at least another thousand. Shoppers came out of the stores that lined the main street to see what was going on. People waiting for buses— that were now delayed because the procession had shut down the street—stood on benches to take photos with their cell phones. Drivers stuck at the intersections got out of their cars, wondering what the heck was going on here.

Bystanders along the way joined in, swept up by the current of the crowd. There were children holding on to the hands of their *abuelas*, toddlers perched on the shoulders of their *tíos*, infants wrapped in the arms of their *mamás*. Aged women walked slowly but fearlessly in the midst of the multitude. With so many people packed into such a small urban space, tragedy could have happened at any moment. Yet we all perceived the need to move gently and deliberately and to watch out for one another so no one was left behind, left out, or harmed.

The servers with the incense, cross, and candles had long moved ahead of us so that we could no longer see them. But we could hear the voice of a cantor who had stationed himself on the back of a flatbed truck at the head of the procession. He was singing through a portable public address system:

"*Santa María Madre de Dios . . .* " and the assembly sang back instinctively, "*Ruega por nosotros.*" Pray for us.

"*San José . . .* " "*Ruega por nosotros.*"

The communion of saints were accompanying us on that road to the cathedral and the holy door. Visitors and neighbors, young and old, families and onlookers, the frail and the strong, the curious, the faithful, and those searching for faith—all of us together, not all understanding what was happening, yet all sensing that something was here, something both mysterious and familiar, around and within and among us, something important and full of meaning.

Here was a chosen race, a royal priesthood, a holy nation, moving step-by-step together on the road, looking out for one another, joining the pilgrimage of the saints to the sanctuary of God. It was at once startling and the most normal thing we could do as Christians on a Sunday. Nick, who had been walking a little behind me, now came up to my side and whispered in my ear, "What if? . . . Just what if this whole year of mercy thing actually works?"

What If We Made Our Parish the Curriculum?

So what if this whole thing actually works? What would happen if we made the RCIA a process that really took place within the community of the faithful?

I believe we'd be making not just new disciples; we would transform our entire parish into a community of disciples and witnesses to Christ.

Whether we knew it or not, the community of Christians on the streets of San José, Costa Rica, that Sunday had become a cloud of witnesses. Our procession was spontaneous, informal, and unrehearsed, but not unplanned. No one had to teach us to be witnesses; someone just said, come, follow, let's sing together. We didn't have to schedule another meeting on our calendar. We just did what we always do on Sundays—gather, pray, listen, give thanks. And as far as I know, none of us were experts in the church's teaching on mercy. But you just had to look at us, a company of strangers, and look at how tenderly we treated one another that day, in simple gestures, to understand what Pope Francis means by creating a revolution of tenderness and mercy.

Those looking for a bit of hope and healing for their wounds, those seeking something more in their life won't find it by studying a text, watching a video, or signing up for a series of classes. But they will find it and more if they just get up and walk alongside us and do what we do until we all get to that holy door together.

The church calls baptism "the door to life and to the kingdom of God" (*Christian Initiation*, General Introduction, 3). The day Rocio stood at our church door, she found more than just a parish. She found a way to the heart of God. Not because we *had* the way all planned out and ready for her, but because we were *on* the way ourselves—the way of Christ—making mistakes and figuring it out, sharing our joy and keeping our hopes set on the one who saves us, begging forgiveness and offering mercy, all the while trusting in the slow, steady, and abiding work of the Spirit.

The day we met Rocio at our door, we found more than just another inquirer. We rediscovered our mission.

If we implement the vision of the RCIA, our parishes will see why baptism matters. When we recognize that baptism in Christ Jesus gives us each mission, we will begin to understand what it means to live as the Body of Christ. If we trust that our baptism gives us everything we need because it gives us one another in Christ, we will find our way together to a door that can change everything.

So come, let's see what if.

Bibliography

Boselli, Goffredo. *The Spiritual Meaning of the Liturgy: School of Prayer, Source of Life*. Translated by Barry Hudock. Collegeville, MN: Liturgical Press, 2014.

Catechism of the Catholic Church. 2nd ed. United States Catholic Conference—Libreria Editrice Vaticana, 1997.

Chesterton, G. K. *What's Wrong with the World*. Mineola, NY: Dover, 2007.

Francis, Pope. Address to Plenary Assembly of the Pontifical Council for Promoting New Evangelization. May 29, 2015. http://w2.vatican.va /content/francesco/en/speeches/2015/may/documents/papa -francesco_20150529_nuova-evangelizzazione.html.

———. The Joy of the Gospel (*Evangelii Gaudium*). Apostolic Exhortation on the Proclamation of the Gospel in Today's World. November 24, 2013. http://w2.vatican.va/content/francesco/en/apost_exhortations /documents/papa-francesco_esortazione-ap_20131124_evangelii -gaudium.html.

———. The Light of Faith (*Lumen Fidei*). Encyclical on Faith. June 29, 2013. http://w2.vatican.va/content/francesco/en/encyclicals/documents /papa-francesco_20130629_enciclica-lumen-fidei.html.

Gray, Mark M. Center for Applied Research in the Apostolate (CARA). *Perspectives from Parish Leaders: U.S. Parish Life and Ministry*. Washington, DC: National Association for Lay Ministry, 2012. http://cara .georgetown.edu/staff/webpages/Parish%20Leaders%20Phase%20 Two.pdf.

Gregory of Nazianzus. *Oratio* 40, 3-4: *Patrologiae cursus completus: Series Graeca* 36, 361C. Quoted in *Catechism of the Catholic Church* 1216.

John Paul II, Pope. Mission of the Redeemer (*Redemptoris Missio*). Encyclical on the Permanent Validity of the Church's Missionary Mandate. December 7, 1990. http://w2.vatican.va/content/john-paul-ii/en/encyclicals/documents/hf_jp-ii_enc_07121990_redemptoris-missio.html.

———. On Catechesis in Our Time (*Catechesi Tradendae*). Apostolic Exhortation. October 16, 1979.

———. Reconciliation and Penance (*Reconciliatio et Paenitentia*). Post-Synodal Apostolic Exhortation. December 2, 1984.

Kavanagh, Aidan. "Christian Initiation in Post-Conciliar Catholicism: A Brief Report." In *Living Water, Sealing Spirit: Readings on Christian Initiation*, edited by Maxwell E. Johnson, 7–8 (Collegeville, MN: Liturgical Press, 1995).

Rite of Christian Initiation of Adults. Study ed. Collegeville, MN: Liturgical Press, 1988.

Spadaro, Antonio. "A Big Heart Open to God: An Interview with Pope Francis." *America*. September 30, 2013. http://www.americamagazine.org/faith/2013/09/30/big-heart-open-god-interview-pope-francis.

United States Conference of Catholic Bishops. *Liturgical Music Today: Guidelines for the Catholic Church Liturgical Musician*. Washington, DC: USCCB, 1982.

———. *Our Hearts Were Burning Within Us: A Pastoral Plan for Adult Faith Formation in the United States*. Washington, DC: USCCB, 1999.

———. *Sing to the Lord: Music in Divine Worship*. Washington, DC: USCCB, 2007.

Vatican II Council. Constitution on the Sacred Liturgy (*Sacrosanctum Concilium*). December 4, 1963. In Austin Flannery, ed., *Vatican Council II: The Conciliar and Postconciliar Documents* (Collegeville, MN: Liturgical Press, 2014).

Vatican II Council. Decree on the Church's Missionary Activity (*Ad Gentes Divinitus*). December 7, 1965. In Austin Flannery, ed., *Vatican Council II: The Conciliar and Postconciliar Documents* (Collegeville, MN: Liturgical Press, 2014).

Wagner, Nick. *Seek the Living God: Five RCIA Inquiry Questions for Making Disciples*. Collegeville, MN: Liturgical Press, 2017.